A Legacy of Ancient Oaks

A Legacy of Ancient Oaks

Mark Frith
Introductory essay by Emma Crichton-Miller

Royal Botanic Gardens Kew

First published in 2018, reprinted 2020,
by the Royal Botanic Gardens, Kew,
Richmond, Surrey, TW9 3AB, UK
www.kew.org

ISBN 978 1 84246 667 4

Distributed on behalf of the Royal Botanic Gardens, Kew in North America by the University of Chicago Press, 1427 East 60th St, Chicago, IL 60637, USA

British Library Cataloguing in Publication Data
A catalogue record for this book is available from the British Library.

Design and page layout: Ocky Murray
Production management: Georgie Hills
Copy-editor and proofreader: Michelle Payne

For information or to purchase all Kew titles please visit
shop.kew.org/kewbooksonline or email publishing@kew.org

Kew's mission is to be the global resource in plant and fungal knowledge, and the world's leading botanic garden.

Kew receives approximately one third of its funding from Government through the Department for Environment, Food and Rural Affairs (Defra).
All other funding needed to support Kew's vital work comes from members, foundations, donors and commercial activities, including book sales.

Printed and bound in Italy by L.E.G.O. S.p.A.

MIX
Paper from responsible sources
FSC www.fsc.org FSC® C023419

The Heart of England Forest
As England's largest new native broadleaf forest, The Heart of England Forest is a registered charity set up to create a 30,000 acre native broadleaf forest for people and for wildlife. The Forest stretches along the Warwickshire / Worcestershire border from south Birmingham, across the Ancient Forests of Arden and Feckenham, to the north Cotswolds. The vision is to plant, protect and preserve a native broadleaf forest – a place of tranquillity and natural beauty that is open to anyone and planted with the help and support of everyone. This national asset provides a lung for the Midlands, and the mosaic of traditional forest habitats aims to increase biodiversity and provide light airy glades and shady canopies for health and relaxation.
www.heartofenglandforest.com

The Heart of England Forest

Winner at the 2019 British Book Design & Production Awards for Exhibition Catalogue

Contents

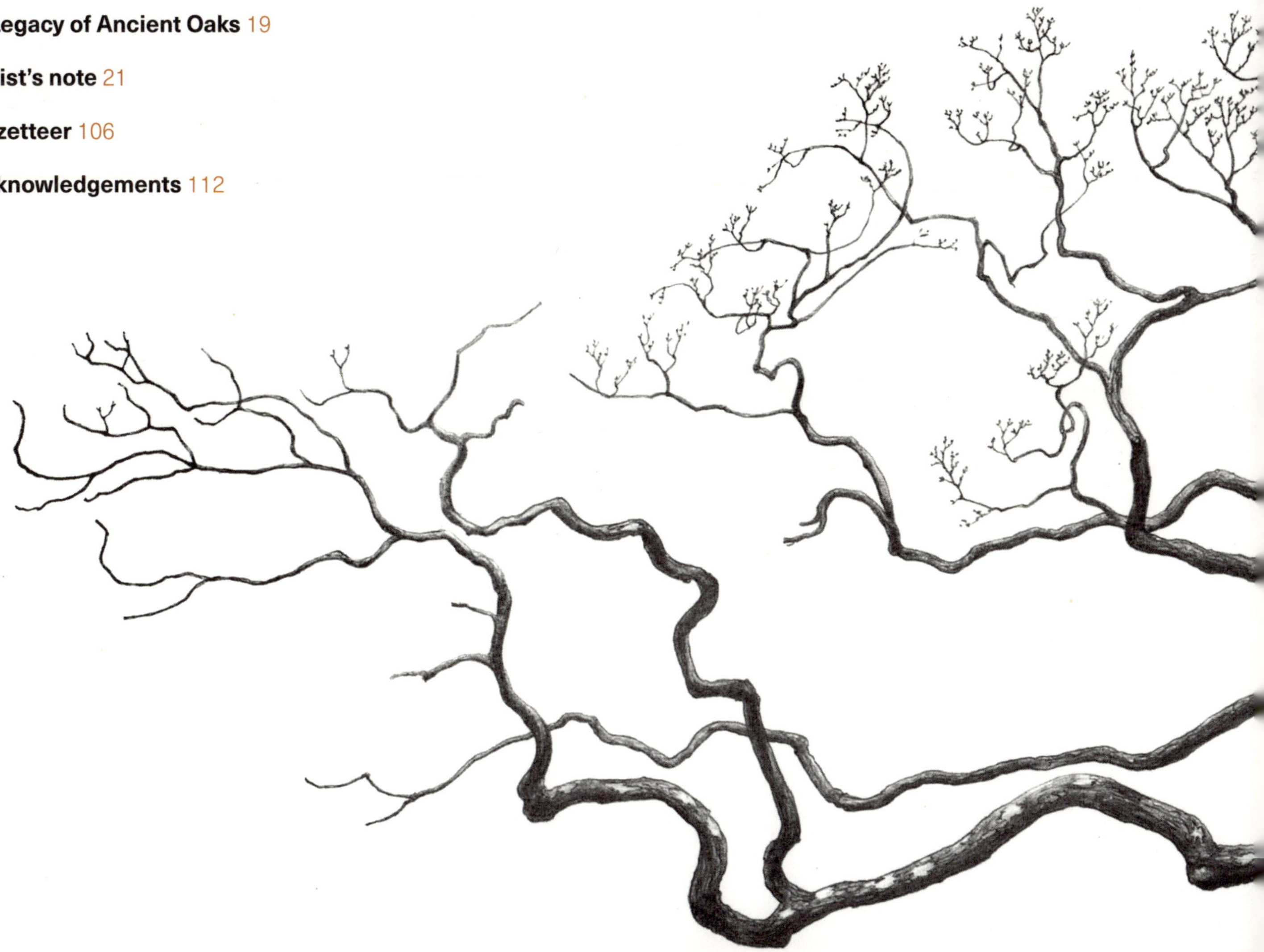

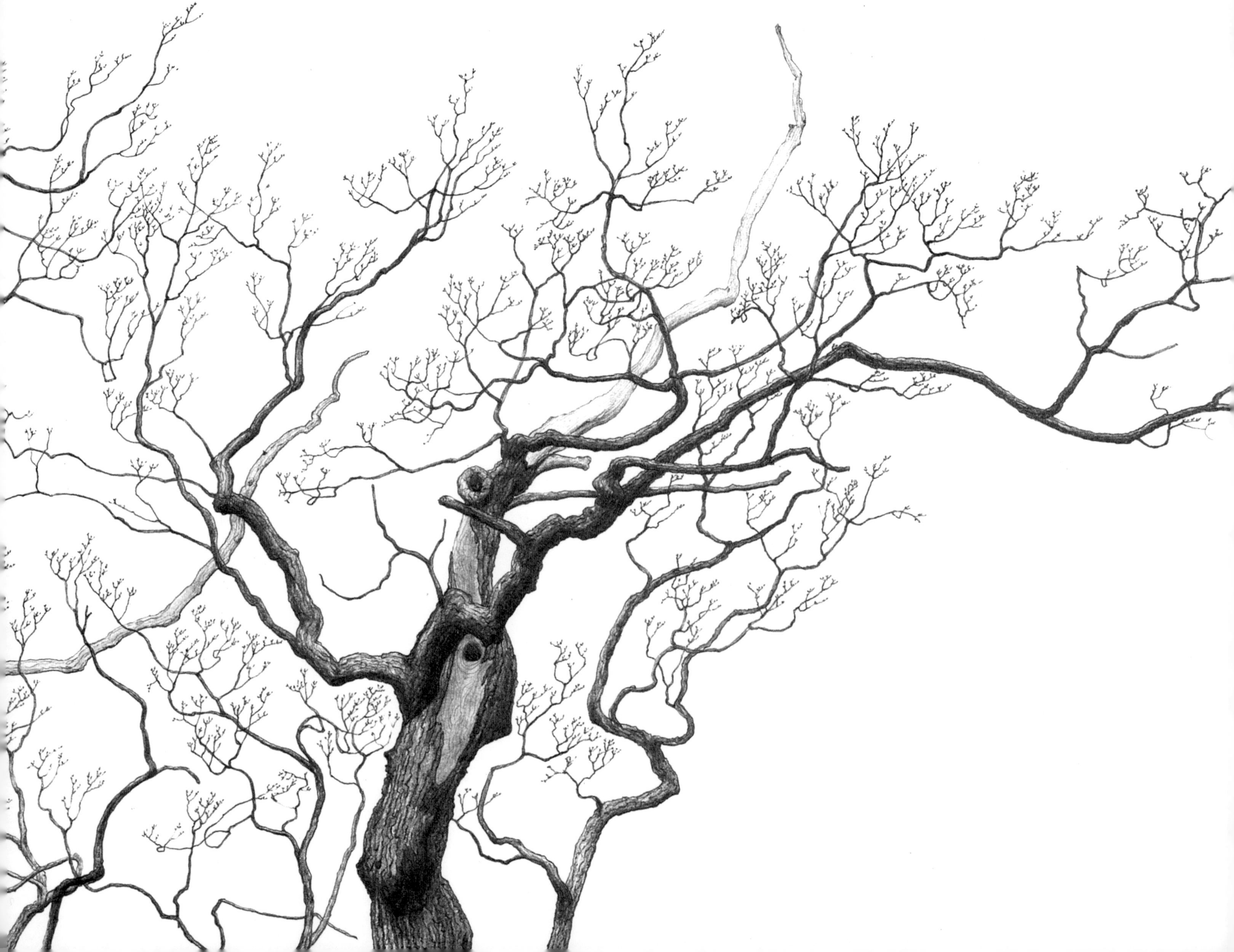

Dedication

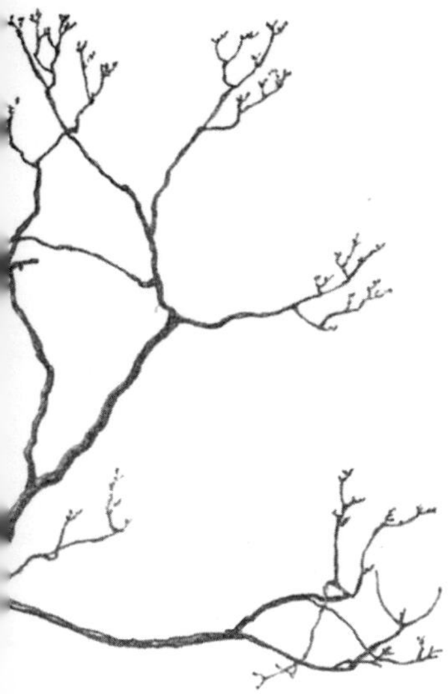

In the autumn of 2010, having spent two months completing the first of what I began to realise must become a series of portraits of Britain's ancient oaks, I knew that such an ambitious project, potentially occupying several years of my life, would not happen without serious financial support. Perhaps, I thought, this end might be achieved by searching out an old fashioned patron. Following a lead from a mutual acquaintance, and staggering under the weight of my first oak tree portrait, I doorstepped the late publisher, poet and lover of trees Felix Dennis at a poetry reading he was giving in Stratford-upon-Avon town hall. Fortunately the drawing spoke for itself and Felix suffered my intrusion enthusiastically. An invitation to lunch followed, during which it became clear that Felix's passion for trees, art and creative endeavour were perfectly aligned with my own ambition to draw the ancient oak portrait series. Lunch ended with Felix scribbling a memorandum confirming his very generous patronage, which he then proceeded to roll up and stuff into the neck of an empty wine bottle. He shoved this across the table, saying 'Show this to your wife, that'll cheer her up!' Then he roared with laughter.

Thus I embarked on a four year journey drawing Britain's ancient oaks, developing, alongside, a parallel acquaintance with a most remarkable man. As an artist's patron, Felix Dennis was without fault. He loved each tree portrait, made no creative demands, laid down no strictures, and simply roared with delighted laughter when, having reached the initially agreed twelve drawings, I suggested we might perhaps go to fourteen, then sixteen and, ultimately, twenty drawings.

Few men have the vision and means to explore their private passions in the way that Felix Dennis did. I learnt that my tree project was modest in comparison with Felix's own, for he was planting a forest. His love of trees had inspired him to create a thirty thousand acre native British forest, open to the public, close to his home in Warwickshire. When I would turn up with two or three more tree portraits to show him, he, having enthusiastically admired the drawings, would regale me with news of a further thousand acres or millionth tree just planted.

Sadly Felix Dennis died in 2014, but before his untimely death he decided on one final patronly act. He donated ten of the twenty drawings to the permanent collection at the Royal Botanic Gardens, Kew. The remaining ten he gave to The Heart of England Forest, the charity created by him, which continues to implement his dream of creating a thirty thousand acre forest. In turn, The Heart of England Forest has lent their ten drawings on a temporary basis to Kew. This book is therefore dedicated to Felix Dennis, without whose extraordinary generosity, vision and creative support this series of ancient oak portraits would not have been completed.

Mark Frith

Drawing trees

Emma Crichton-Miller

In the British Museum, among the stone slabs that once graced the throne room of the powerful Neo-Assyrian King Ashurnasirpal II (ruler from 883–859 BC), there is a large shallow relief carving of a schematic tree. Either side of the tree stands an image of the King together with a winged guardian, while above a winged disc hovers, representing the god Aššur. The tree is rendered as a symmetrical patterned network of nodes and branches, with flourishing leaves at the end of each branch and a crown or headdress of palm leaves. By the time Ashurnasirpal's dexterous and subtle sculptors carved this image, the tree was already an ancient symbol. For two millennia this emblem, known today as the Tree of Life, had been used by the people of the region to signify the King's sacred connection to the current of life running from the earth, through the tree to a divine power.

The carving is a drawing in stone. It takes us back to the primeval roots of our identification with trees, our recognition that they embody more abundantly than any other life form the fertility of our earth and its generative power. The tree links us also to the heavens, reaching up so high above us to appeal for clement weather and fruitful rain, responding to every whisper of wind or change of season, whilst offering us shelter from blizzards, downpours or unyielding sunlight. Whether it is because we are descended from tree dwellers or because *Homo sapiens* lived for so long in symbiosis with these giant creatures, they continue to inspire in us a mixture of empathy and awe.

When Mark Frith returned to his childhood home in Gloucestershire, in 2007, it was the trees in the landscape that moved him to draw. A film-maker for many years, he had originally trained as an artist, with a childhood of drawing behind him. The landscape of the Berkeley Vale, rolling gently from the falling edge of the Cotswold scarp to the River Severn, is marked out by mature trees. Some of these grace ancient parkland; others indicate boundaries and hedge-lines. Either way, it is through trees that this landscape is articulated, with the oak and ash bringing to life the underlying contours and the overlaying field patterns, offering shape, rhythm and colour. 'It was autumn and winter when we moved back into this house,' Frith recalls, 'and the trees were everywhere, impressive and handsome. I saw an oak tree I used to climb as a boy just behind my house and one day I simply started to draw it.'

The project which ensued – to draw a series of portraits of Britain's most significant ancient oak trees – fits within a distinct tradition of art. It is not quite botanical drawing, where what matters above all is the scientific accuracy of the depiction of twig, bud, leaf, flower and fruit, with the mighty tree itself left to the imagination. Nor is it quite landscape art, where trees become the sinuous frames to distant vistas or one of many compositional elements within a broader conjuring of a sense of place. For millennia artists have been drawn to the tree as a subject in its own right: whether those ancient Assyrians carving a highly schematic Tree of Life

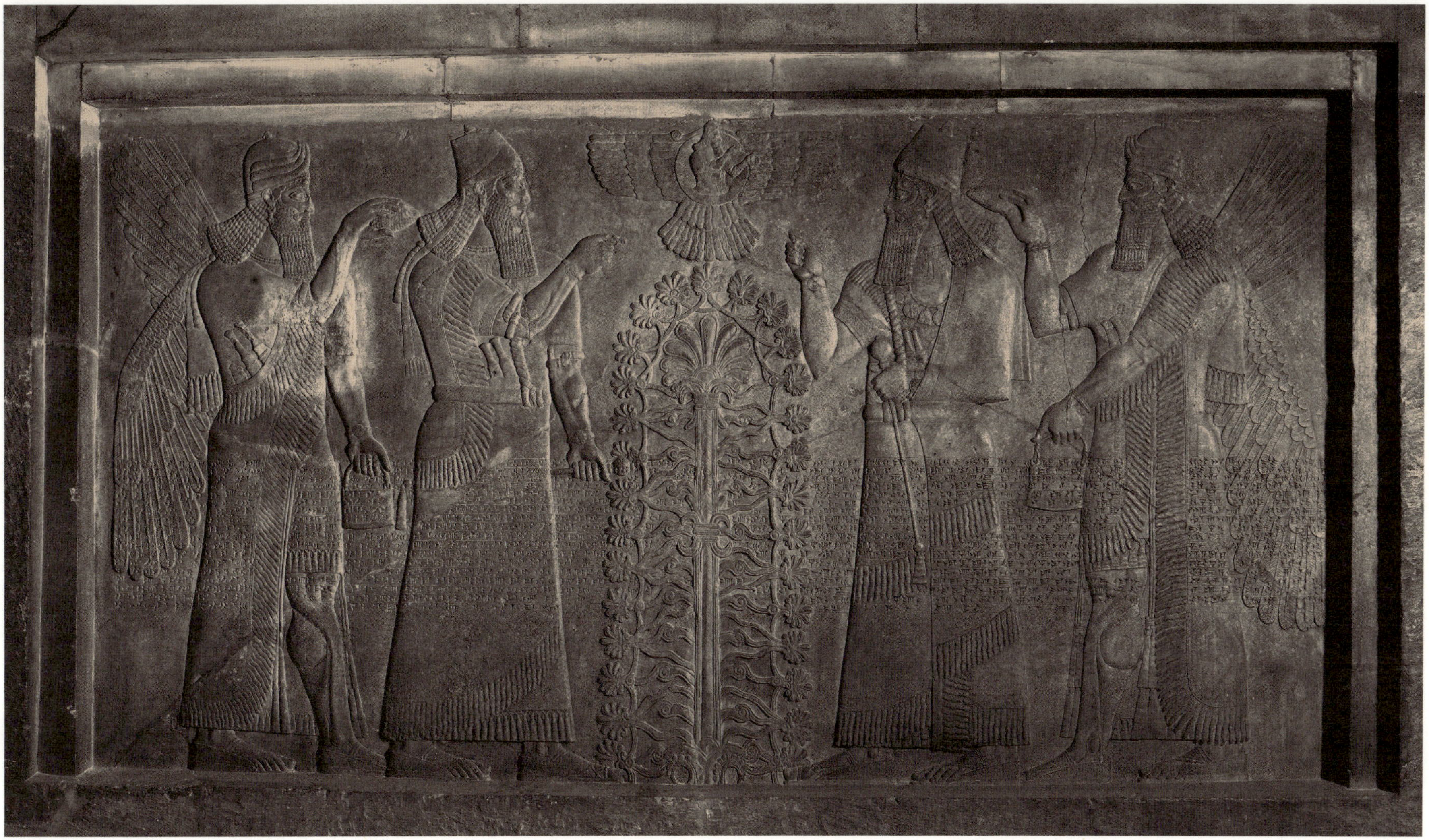

Wall panel showing the Tree of Life, Neo-Assyrian, c. 865–860 BC. © The Trustees of the British Museum

or Van Gogh expressing with his pencil his love for pollarded willows and birches, for cherry trees and cypresses. These range from the highly symbolic to the highly naturalistic through to the highly Romantic, where it is the artist's identification with the tree, the personalisation of it, that is paramount. Mark Frith's drawings fit within this last category. He uses his pencil as a means of conjuring, through empathy, the soul of particular trees, as a way of acknowledging our kinship with them and our long intertwined destinies. As significant works of art, however, they inevitably carry within them the whole history of man's creative response to trees.

The European story

In the earliest surviving depictions of trees their symbolic significance is paramount. The trees dotting the paradisal landscapes of the sixth-century mosaics in the Church of Sant'Apollinare in Classe in Ravenna, with their varieties of schematic leafage, reflect the original Eden. We respond to them as if they were trees in a dream of perfection, remote from our world. Throughout the medieval period, the idea of the single Tree of Life becomes entwined with the notion of the Tree of Knowledge in the Garden of Eden, and also with other Biblical ideas such as the Tree of Jesse, tracing the descent of Jesus, and the Tree of Redemption, or the cross. These feature in exuberant colour in books of hours, illuminated Bibles or mosaics.

It was the early Italian painter, Giotto di Bondone, in thirteenth and fourteenth century Florence, who first sought to give these scriptural trees more local resonance, modelling his still schematic versions on Tuscan trees set amidst Tuscan hills. This was the first hint of the swerve to naturalism in art that was to occur during the Renaissance. As John Ruskin wrote in the nineteenth century, 'in the one principle of close imitation of nature lay Giotto's great strength and the entire secret of the revolution he effected.' Giotto's famous fresco of the Sermon to the Birds, a part of the Legend of Saint Francis cycle in the Basilica in Assisi, was completed c.1297–1299. This tree, with its asymmetric trunk and exuberant foliage, is undoubtedly as powerful a figure as the Saint and his companion. The tree seems to lean forward to listen also to the sermon the Saint is delivering to the birds, which cluster around its foot as if it were their protector.

It is with Leonardo da Vinci, however, that naturalism becomes dominant. Amongst his many drawings held in the Royal Collection there is a delicate study in red chalk of a slender elm tree dating from around 1500. Here it is the tree for its own sake, and the chalk's capacity to direct the artist's looking, to interrogate and bring to life the tree's particular nature, that matters. Underneath the drawing da Vinci has written, in his coded mirror writing, a note about the different appearance of leaves in sunlight and in shadow. This coming together of forensic scrutiny of the visible world and art was one principle mark of the Italian Renaissance. It was no longer necessary always to look at nature through the lens of religion. Nature could tell its own stories. Key to this storytelling power, as the great early twentieth-century German art historian Wilhelm Worringer remarks of Renaissance art in general, is the artist's act of empathy. What matters most is not absolute accuracy but that the drawing projects 'the lines and forms of the organically vital, the euphony of its rhythm and its whole inward being, outward . . . for the free, unimpeded activation of one's own sense of life.' We feel our own life, our bond with this tree, through the liveliness of this drawing.

In the Netherlands and Flanders, a parallel turn towards naturalism saw the emergence of a distinct school of landscape painting, initially as a backdrop to Biblical storytelling, but gradually as a genre in itself. In the drawings of Pieter Bruegel the Elder, especially, it is so often a magnificent tree that dominates –

Verso: ***A tree*** **c.1500–10 by Leonardo da Vinci.** Royal Collection Trust / © Her Majesty Queen Elizabeth II 2018

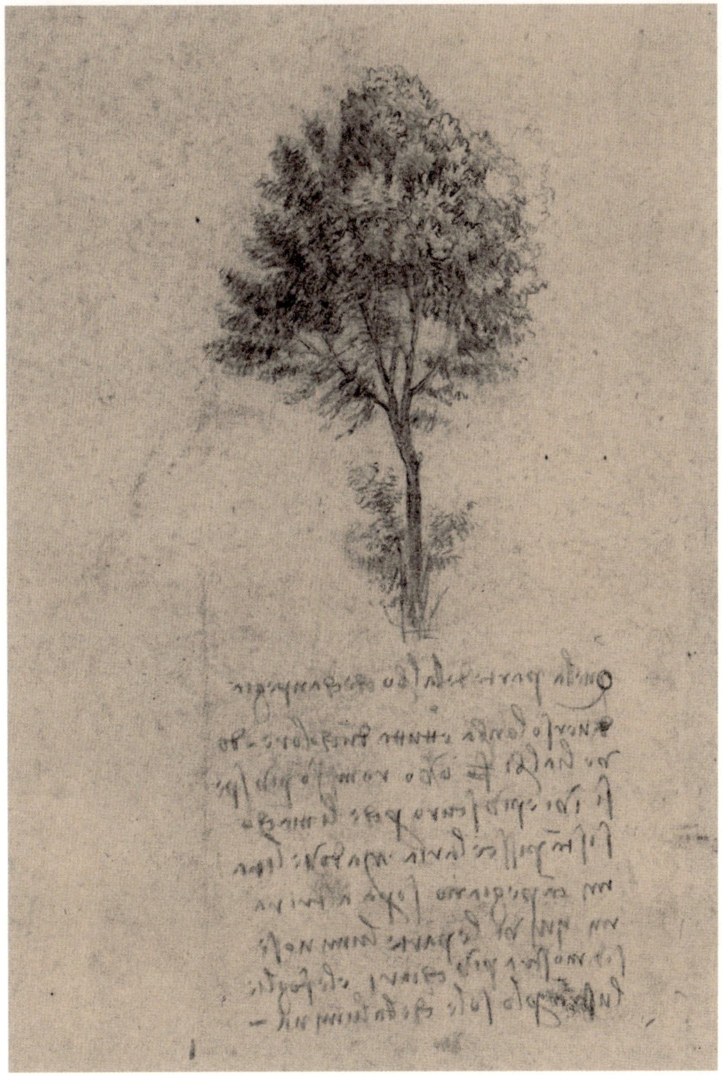

vigorously twisting and turning, with sinewy branches – leaving other figures in the composition, the people and animals, very much secondary.

For Jacob von Ruisdael, one of the leading Dutch landscape artists of the following century, closely observed trees became dramatic actors in his atmospheric landscapes, suggesting a more Romantic approach to landscape. Applying heavier paint than his predecessors, Ruisdael gave his foliage a rich, sappy quality, suggestive of the tree's vigour rising from root to top. Mood and atmosphere are paramount in his paintings, but he also brought a scientific accuracy of vision to bear on his paintings of different trees: even today botanists can identify precisely the genera depicted. Ruisdael was a key influence on the British school of landscape painting which would emerge during the eighteenth century, and from which Frith is ultimately descended.

Another significant figure for British artists in the eighteenth century was the wild, Naples-born Salvator Rosa (1615–1673), with his storm-tossed trees in rocky landscapes. The Metropolitan Museum of Art in New York holds a wonderful drawing by him of a single large tree. This monumental drawing measures 61.5 x 41.8 cm and is unusual for focusing entirely on a single tree (p12), isolated from any broader narrative or landscape context. It seems to dance up from the base, balancing its vigorous, carefully drawn, twisting limbs with their festoons of leaves, and rising to a sunlit shock of foliage. This is a quintessentially Romantic portrait of a single tree, summoning for the viewer a sense of its unique arboreal life.

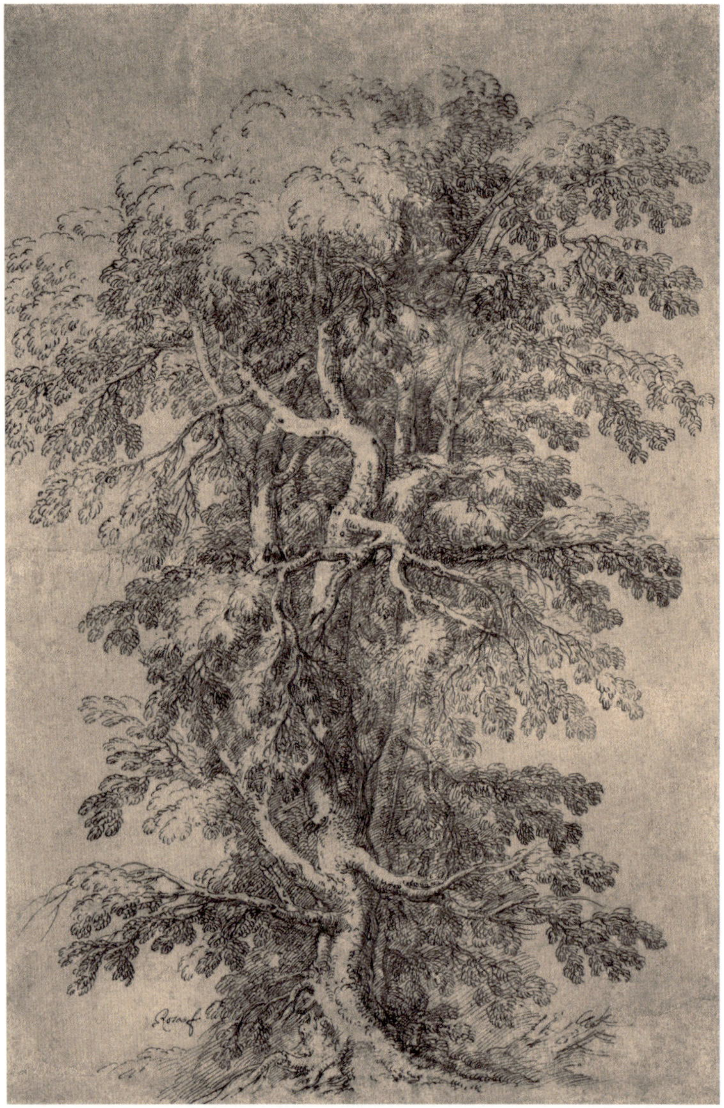

A Large Tree by Salvator Rosa (1615–1673). © Rogers Fund, 1911

as deeply as Claude; we know that he boasted of carefully recording the specific features of each one and yet he articulates their branches in a random, utterly careless way.' But for three centuries English collectors, writers, poets and artists have loved Claude's depictions of trees for the way he shows their animated swags of leaves catching the various lights of dawn, midday and sunset: as J. M. W. Turner put it, 'trees possessing every hue and tone of summer's evident heat, rich, harmonious, true and clear ...'

The English story

When the landed gentry of England began to transform the English landscape at the beginning of the eighteenth century, Claude was their guide. Newly confident of their role in British life following the Glorious Revolution of 1688, the building of grand country houses went hand in hand with elaborate landscaping schemes. William Kent, Lancelot 'Capability' Brown and Humphrey Repton were hired to recreate on English turf the painted landscapes of Claude, Rosa and Nicolas Poussin, which their patrons had encountered on the Grand Tour. Besides sweeping parkland, managed woodland and the proud foregrounding

The individual artist most influential upon the distinctly British school of landscape painting, however, was the Frenchman Claude Lorrain, renowned for his golden-lit pastoral and mythological scenes. He was not necessarily an expert draughtsman: in 1924 Roger Fry wrote rather disdainfully: 'one can bet that nobody loved trees

of venerable trees was a primary aesthetic. In turn, Thomas Gainsborough, among many other British artists, painted his more recently landed clients under spreading trees to reinforce their association with an ancient, settled British order, while George Stubbs took as much loving care with the trees of his patrons as with their brood mares, prize foals and beloved hunters.

The depiction of trees in Britain has also been influenced by a specific cultural history of trees. For centuries, trees and woodland were fraught symbols of royal power, preserved by the King for his own recreation, but also the home of sturdy resistant woodlanders who regarded the forests as their natural patrimony. Most of the trees which Frith has drawn stand within the remnants of medieval deer parks, many of which originated as royal hunting grounds with trees protected from early demise by King's decree. It is no surprise that the artist Anthony van Dyck painted Charles I on horseback surveying his kingdom beneath a spreading oak tree. The restoration of Charles II and the Stuart Monarchy in 1660 reasserted the association between royalty and woodland: after all, Charles II had notoriously escaped Cromwell's forces by hiding in an oak tree, after his defeat at the battle of Worcester in 1651. John Evelyn, a staunch royalist, named the returning King Nemorensis Rex, meaning King of the Grove, and in 1664 published the most famous book on forestry ever written: *Sylva, Or a Discourse of Forest Trees, and the Propagation of Timber in His Majesties Dominions*. Trees became a matter of patriotism, planted to provide masts and hulls for ships in the foreign wars and mercantile adventures that marked the eighteenth century.

The oak

In choosing to draw the oak, in particular, Frith reflects a distinctly British fondness. Through the eighteenth century Britain's identity became entwined with this native deciduous tree, dominant in English woodland for over 8,000 years. Lines from Virgil, Homer and other classical and contemporary poets were frequently quoted to emphasise the tree's resilience, the wide spread of its branches and its deep roots in the past. John Evelyn reported an oak in Worksop Park belonging to the Duke of Norfolk 'under the shade whereof near a thousand horses might commodiously stand at once.' A revived fascination with Druids, for whom the oak was sacred, identified the trees with a pure and original ancient British culture. The Seven Years War (1756–1763), during which Britain trounced France and Spain at sea, inspired another round of patriotic fervour, and the publication of Roger Fisher's report *Heart of Oak: The British Bulwark*, encouraging more tree planting, and a new edition of Evelyn's *Sylva*. Meanwhile, the carnage of the French Revolution sealed British political philosopher Edmund Burke's emotional identification of English conservatism with the oak, the 'British oak' representing a society that has grown organically, a slowly evolving and stable national community.

If the oak served politically, it also had aesthetic qualities that set it apart. The Reverend William Gilpin, one of the originators of the idea of 'the picturesque' in landscape, elucidated at great length in his book *Remarks on Forest Scenery, and other woodland Views* (1791) that among individual trees, the oak is 'both the most picturesque tree in itself, and the most accommodating in composition.' Chief amongst the qualities that make it attractive to an artist, he suggests, is the way its limbs twist, and 'like the course of a river, sport and play in every possible direction – sometimes in longer stretches, and sometimes in shorter elbows.' Gilpin also notes that the spray of the oak follows the pattern of its branches, often ramifying abruptly at right angles: 'hence the spray of the Oak becomes thick, close and interwoven; so that, at a little distance, it has a full, rich, appearance, and more of the picturesque roughness than we observe in the spray of any other tree.'

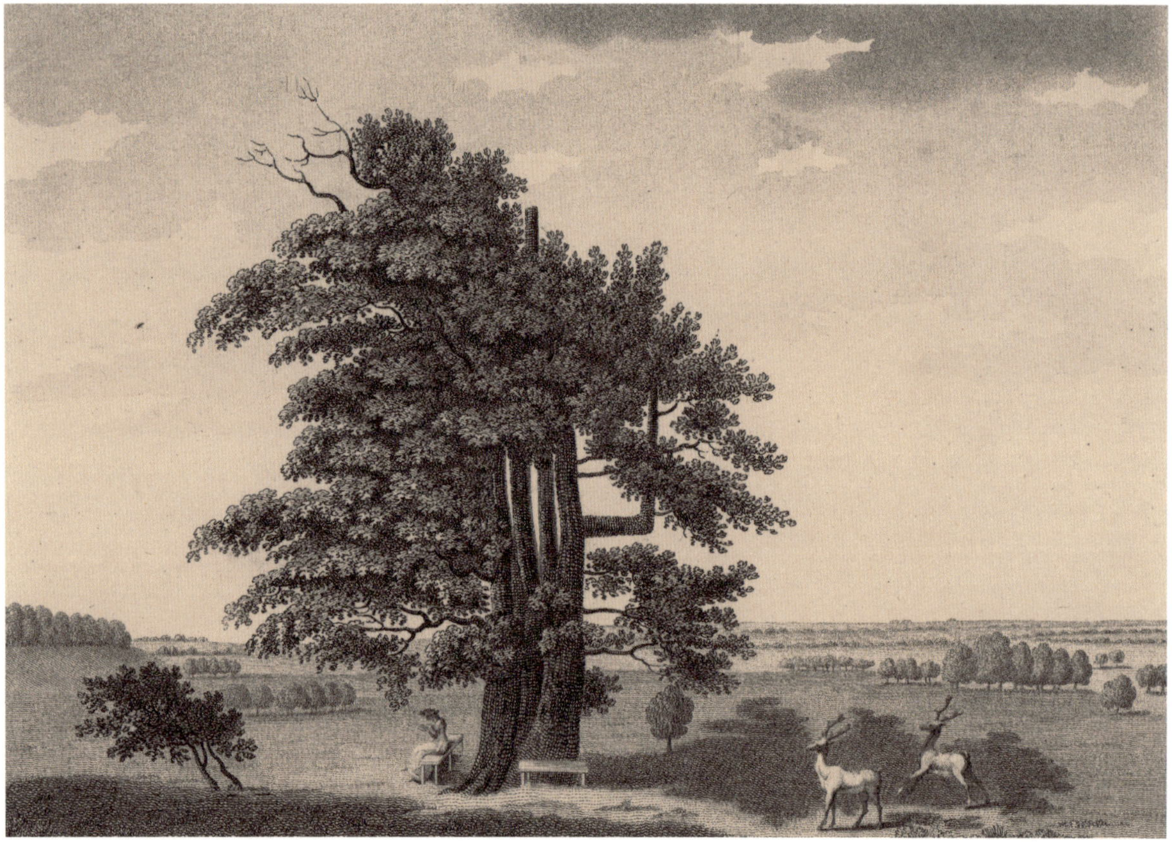

The Seven Sisters by Hayman Rooke from *Descriptions and Sketches of Some Remarkable Oaks in the Park at Wellbeck, in the County of Nottingham* by Henry William Burgess, 1790.

But if the oak in general was admired, so increasingly, were individual specimens, with artists seeking out especially those of great age or historical significance. Frith is certainly not the first to have embarked on a series of individual portraits. In 1790 Hayman Rooke, sponsored by his patron the Duke of Portland, published *Descriptions and Sketches of Some Remarkable Oaks in the Park at Wellbeck, in the County of Nottingham*. He records that he made his drawings of the Greendale Oak and the Seven Sisters in 1779, but 'that drawings of the green dale oak in several views of it, had been made, several years before 1779, by Grim and others.'

A fascination with the ancient trees which marked the countryside, and which were indeed listed in guidebooks, reached a peak in the 1820s. In 1827 Henry William Burgess published *Eidodendron*, a collection of lithographs realised after his drawings, or *Views of the general Character and Appearance of Trees foreign and indigenous as connected with picturesque scenery*. He complained that botanists too often study a sprig, leaf or bud, 'neglecting the

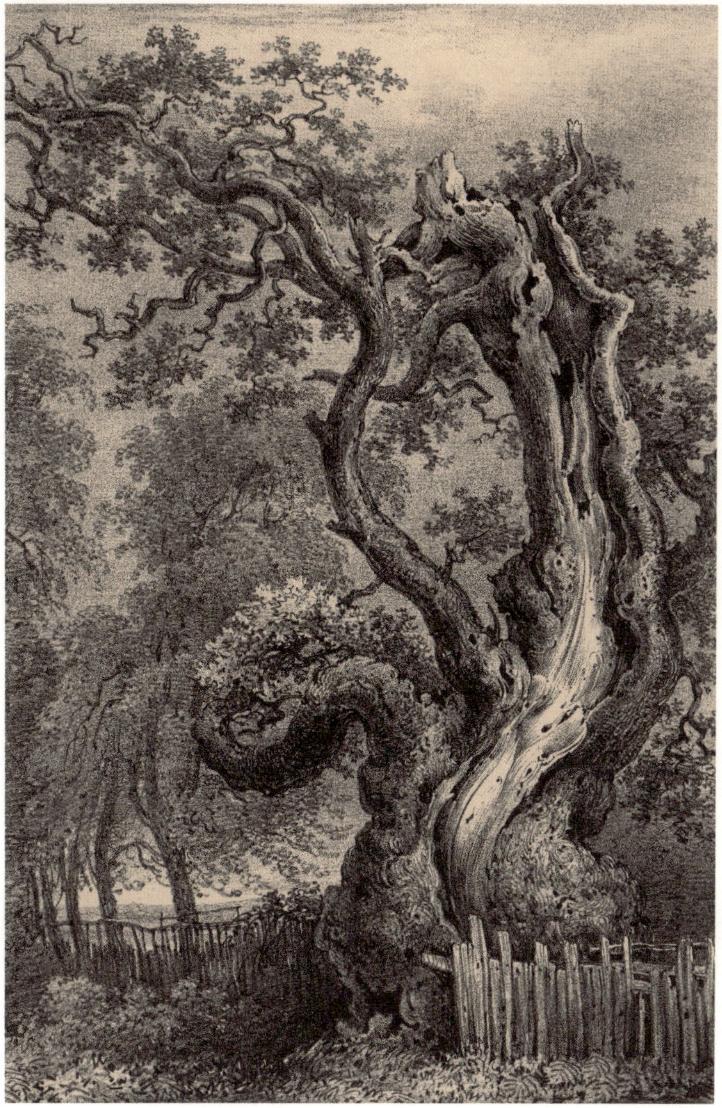

The King Oak from *Eidodendron* by Henry William Burgess, 1827. © RBG Kew

higher and more philosophic task of contemplating the stupendous grandeur of the whole.' Burgess's trees are also vividly characterised with writhing trunks and dramatic contrasts of sunlight and shadow.

One year earlier Thomas Strutt had published his landmark collection *Sylva Britannica or Portraits of Forest Trees*, which he dedicated to John, Duke of Bedford. He opens with the same Greendale Oak at Wellbeck – spectacular for the carriageway cut into its trunk – depicted by Hayman Rooke. Strutt draws twenty individual oaks and then the Seven Sisters at Burghley, an oak with seven parallel trunks springing from one base, conjuring their immensity and relishing with his pen their many knobbly, gnarled differences. As he puts it, 'to the casual observer of nature the view of one tree may seem much like the view of another; and that a forest itself is more calculated to strike the imagination by the greatness of its aggregate, than to interest it by the variety of its detail: but it is very different with the ardent contemplatist of Nature'. This nature-lover, he goes on, 'loves to trace in each individual specimen, its peculiar anatomy and character. Every winding branch, and every shooting stem, has a charm for him; and he is interested throughout each stage of the existence of these wonder vegetable structures, from the tender sapling, to the leafless withered trunk.'

Above all, Strutt is impressed by the Great Oak at Fredville, also known as Majesty, with its enormous trunk and spiralling sequence of branches. Together with the nearby oaks Beauty and Stately it forms a group, 'which for magnificence and beauty, is not perhaps exceeded by any other of the same nature.' It was in a similar spirit of awe that Frith first approached the Fredville Oak, nearly two hundred years later. Indeed, one reason behind Frith's decision to focus entirely on the bare structure of the winter tree – abstracted from context, without background

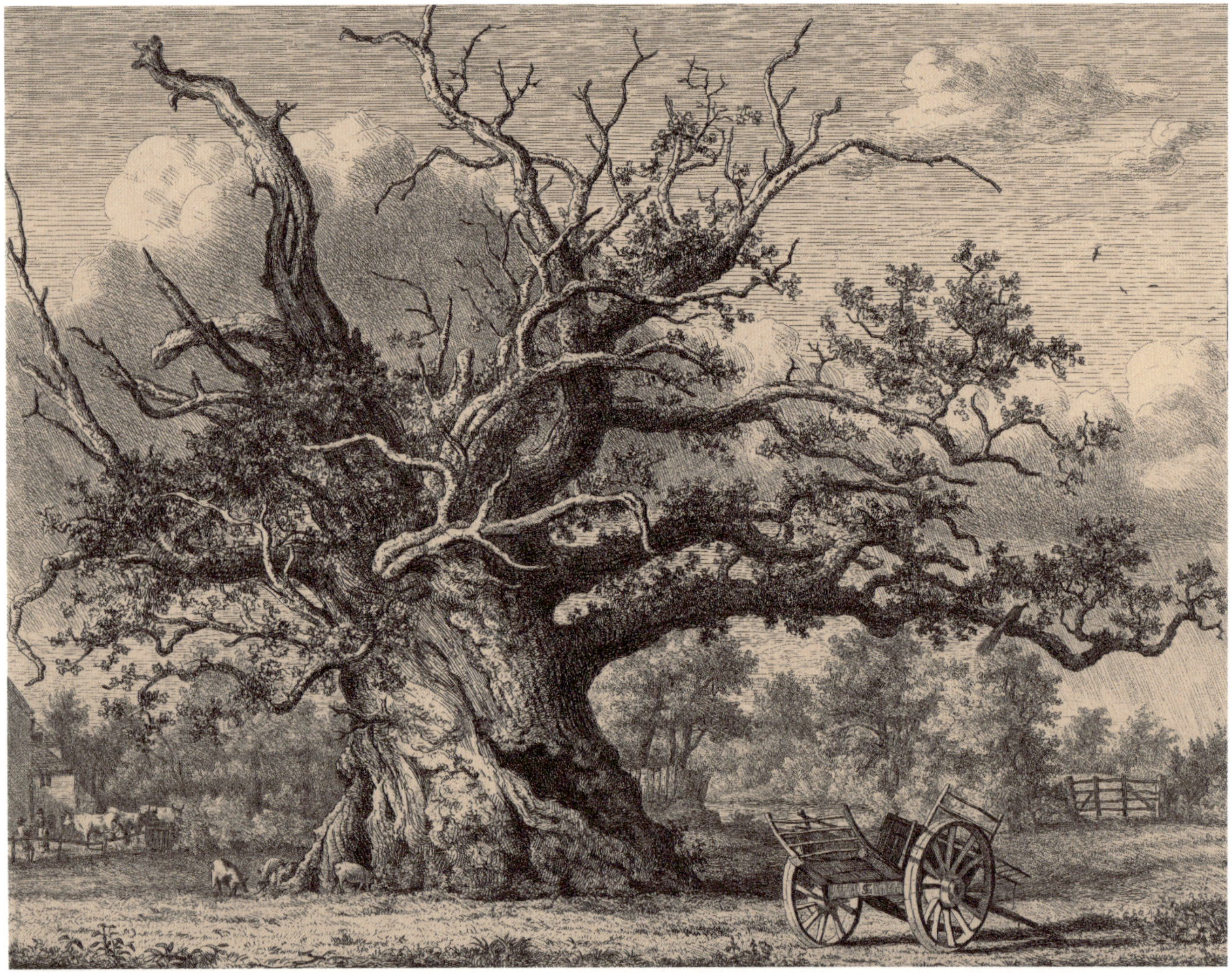

The Cowthorpe Oak from *Sylva Britannica* by Jacob George Strutt, 1826. © RBG Kew

or foliage, and quite unlike the trees of Strutt, Burgess or Rooke – was to better honour, in a contemporary idiom, each 'peculiar anatomy.' The use of graphite on white paper enables him, with a variety of different strokes, to render every twig and gnarl. As he says, 'the texture of the bark and the muscularity of the oak tree in winter, all of that appeals very strongly to somebody drawing, and it comes alive to the pencil on the paper.' But as well as accuracy, Frith wanted to capture the less tangible personality of these giant inhabitants of our landscape, adjusting the composition of parts to convey better the spirit of the whole. Key to this, and to the impact of his drawings, is their scale. Just as the trees astonish visitors with their size, so these drawings amaze by the combination of their size and the intricate detail that holds viewers' attention both from a distance and even when they are standing close up.

The Great Oak at Fredville from *Sylva Britannica* by Jacob George Strutt, 1826.

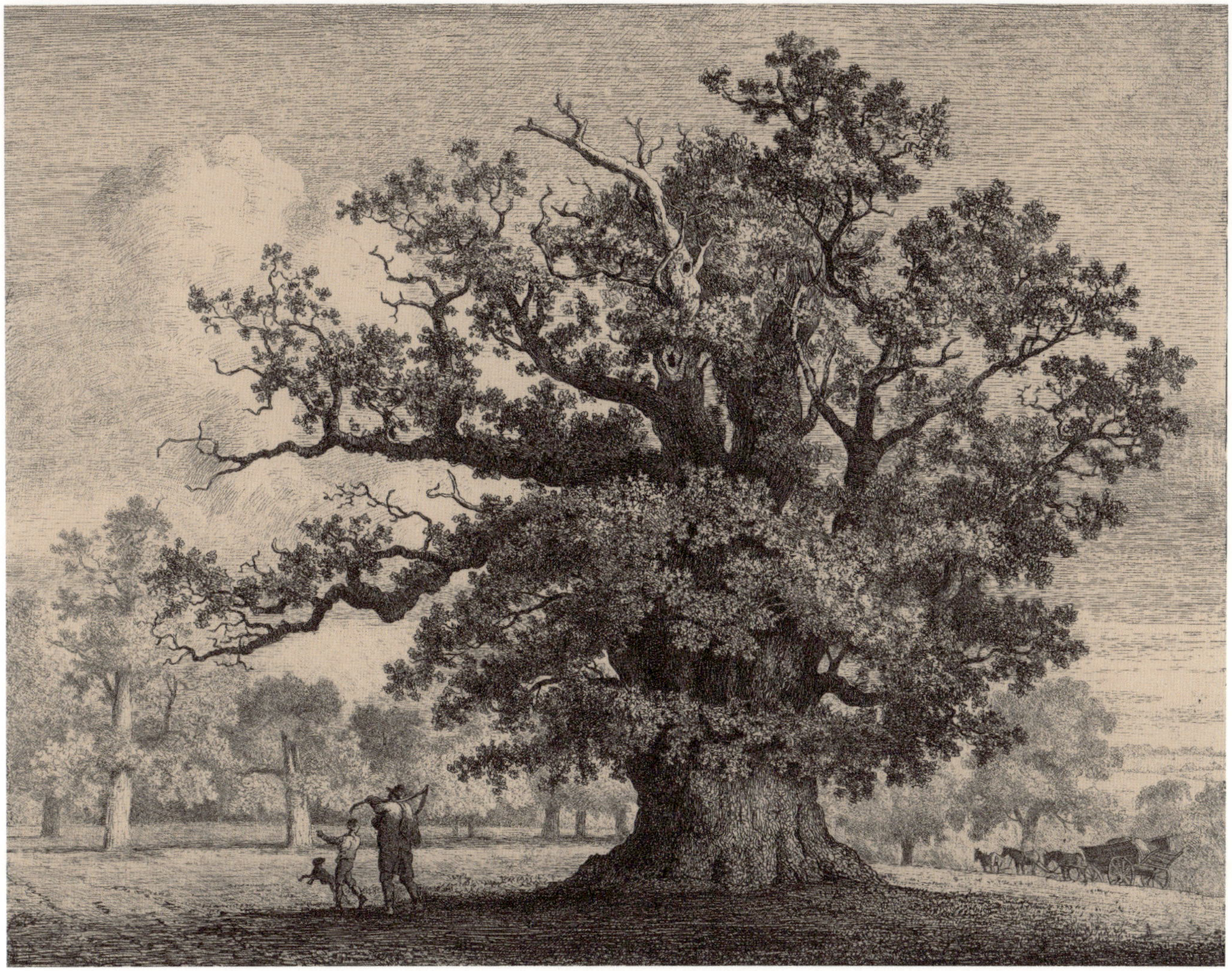

While these individual portraits of mighty trees seek to honour their venerable particularity, as he progressed Frith became increasingly committed to the series as a historic enterprise. Nearly two hundred years after Strutt, the drawings create a twenty-first century record of the most significant still standing ancient oaks. These awe-inspiring trees are under threat from climate change and imported diseases, as much as from the storms and droughts they have already weathered. These survivors are the sentinels of our future. They bear witness to the travails of the past but also respond acutely to assaults from our contemporary environment, which is shared by every living creature. Frith's drawings encourage us to look on these kings of the forest as fellow beings, which are thrilling in their longevity and resilience but ultimately as vulnerable as flesh and blood.

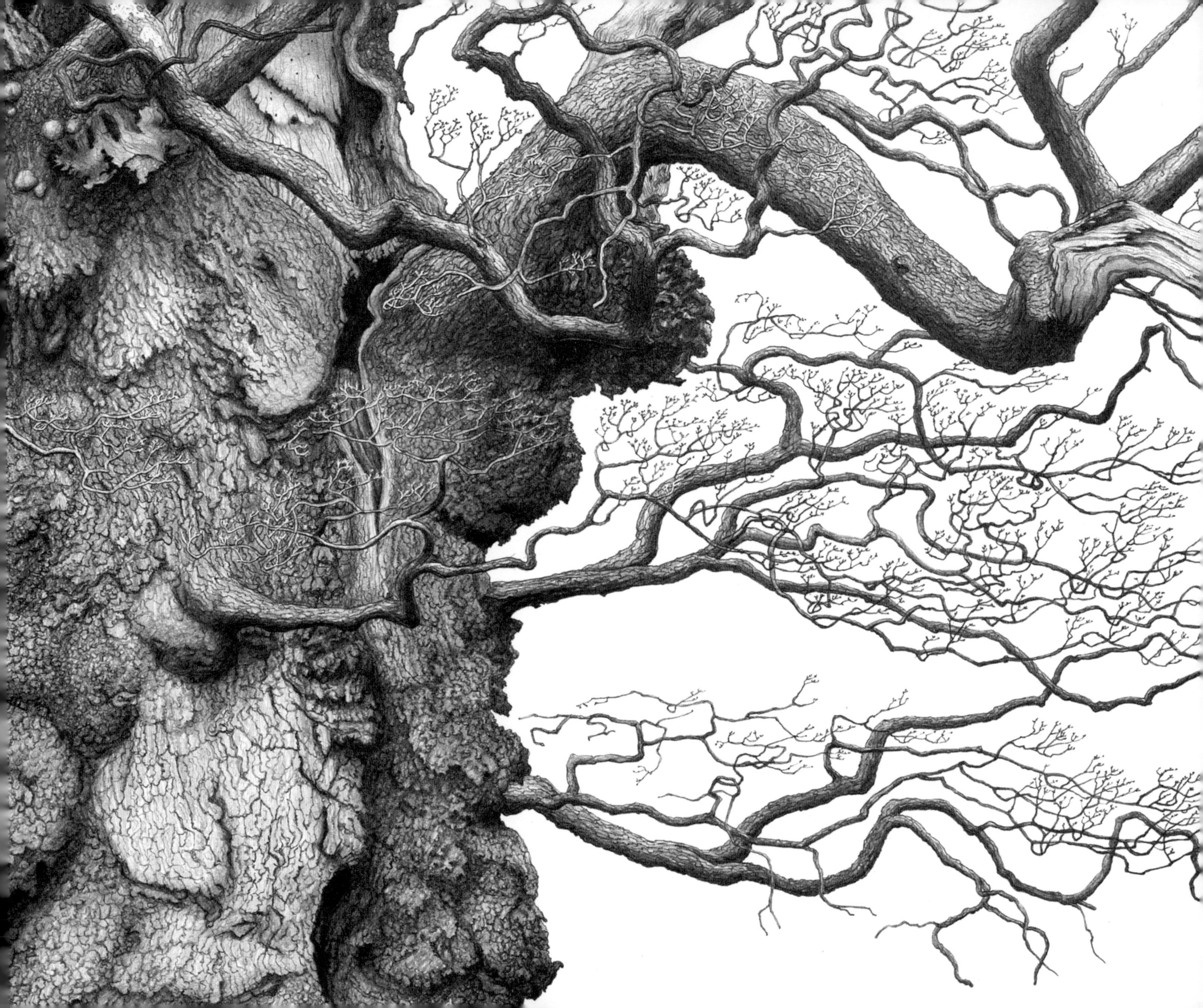

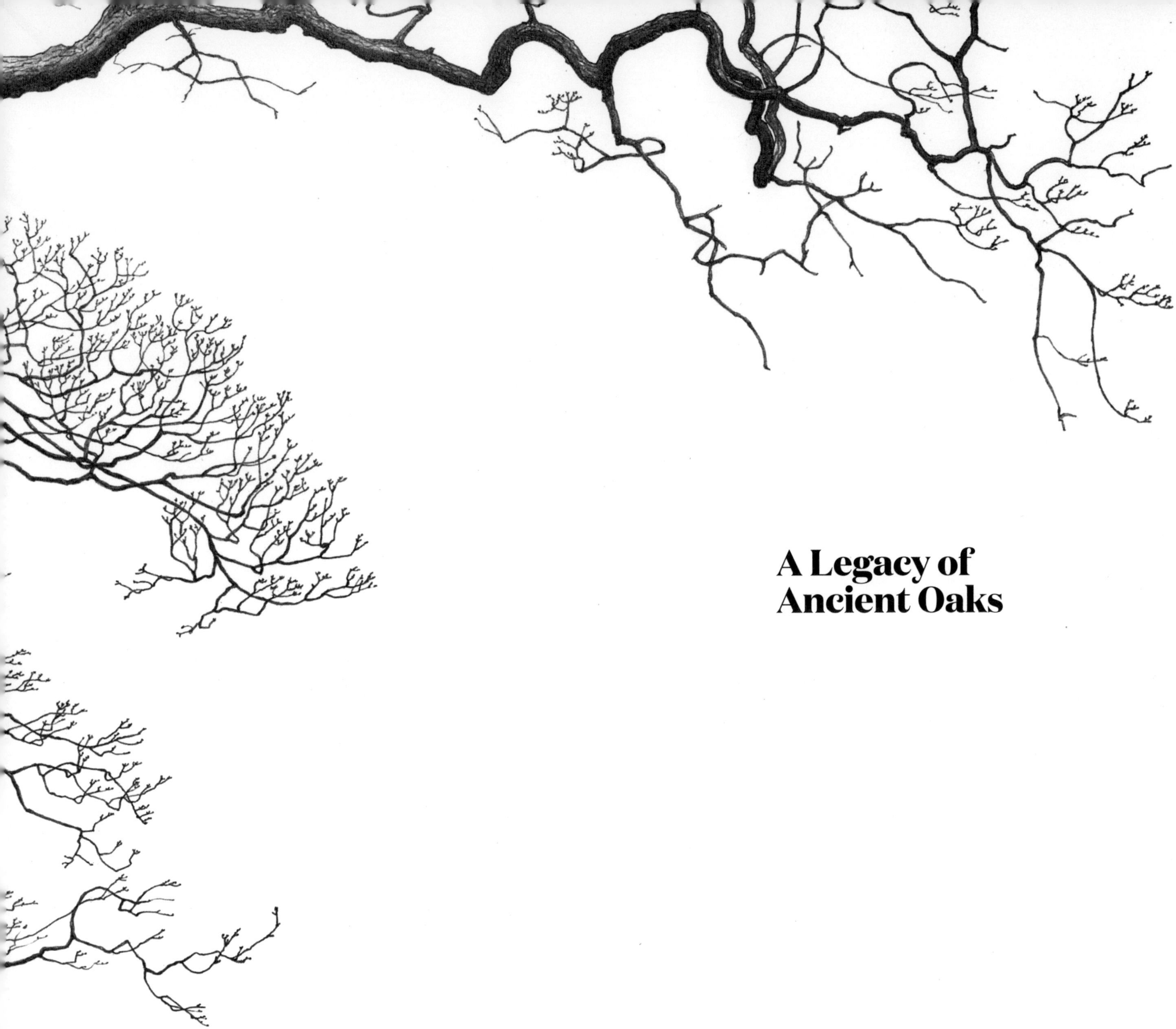

A Legacy of Ancient Oaks

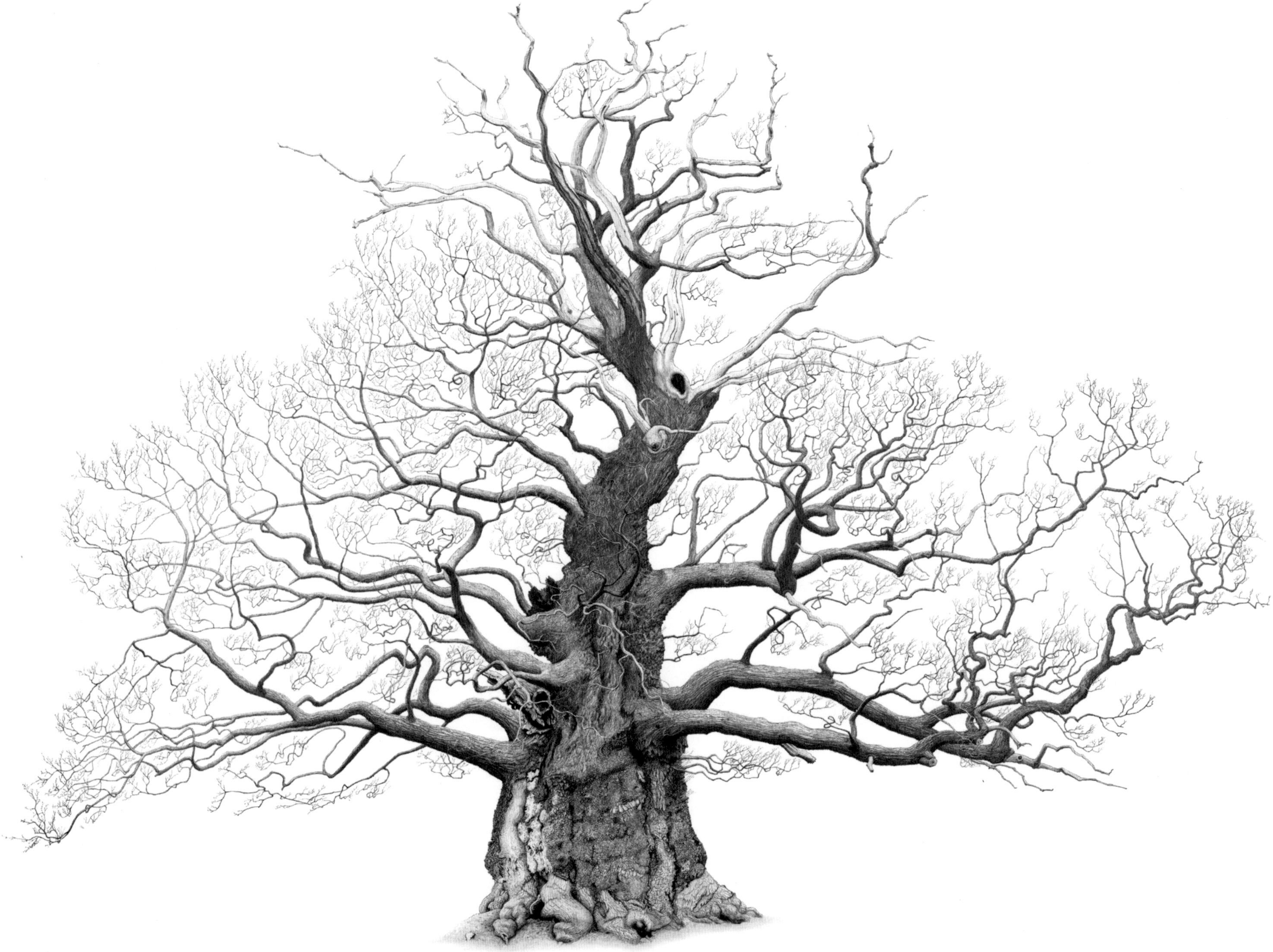

Artist's note

Fortune gave me a boyhood of unfettered wandering amongst hedgerow, hay meadow and woodland, deep in the English countryside. Aimless days whose sole purpose, it seemed, was to avoid the tiresome attentions of the adult world whilst plundering the many wonders of the natural one.

Dreaming my way through greenwood and grassland I stumbled across one of the major characters of the locality, the Great Oak at Nibley Green. A fantastical giant, impossibly old, a treasure trove filled with wonder enough to overflow my young imagination. Inside and out, up and down, in the company of jackdaws, foxes, mice, barn owls, beetles and bats I explored bark, bough, twig, leaf, acorn and the mouldering, cavernous hollow interior of that ancient tree. No surprise then that the first tree I should ever draw, in 2010, was that same Great Oak at Nibley Green.

I embarked on the drawing with no great purpose other than that, finding myself living back in my childhood home, the tree was there. Gradually, over the two months spent working on the drawing I became aware of a curious sensation – at times the tree appeared to draw itself. My hand would move over the paper at a remove from my conscious mind. At the same time I seemed to feel the twigs, the texture of the bark, the weight of the branches. I could even smell the mouldering decay of the hollow interior. Allied to these curious sensations was a sense that the overall image in the drawing came from somewhere beyond the tree in front of me – as of course it did. That dreaming boy had become father to the man.

This sensation of almost automatic drawing was repeated over and over again as I worked on this series of ancient oak portraits. I owe a debt of thanks then to that small boy, whose aimless wanderings and untutored learning has come to fruition in this series of drawings. Drawings that I hope in some modest way express man's profound relationship with the natural world and, if it has one, something of the soul of the ancient oak tree.

Mark Frith

The Great Oak at Nibley Green
Gloucestershire
Quercus robur
Graphite on paper
150 × 120 cm
2010

The Marton Oak
Cheshire
Quercus petraea
Graphite on paper
150 × 120 cm
2011

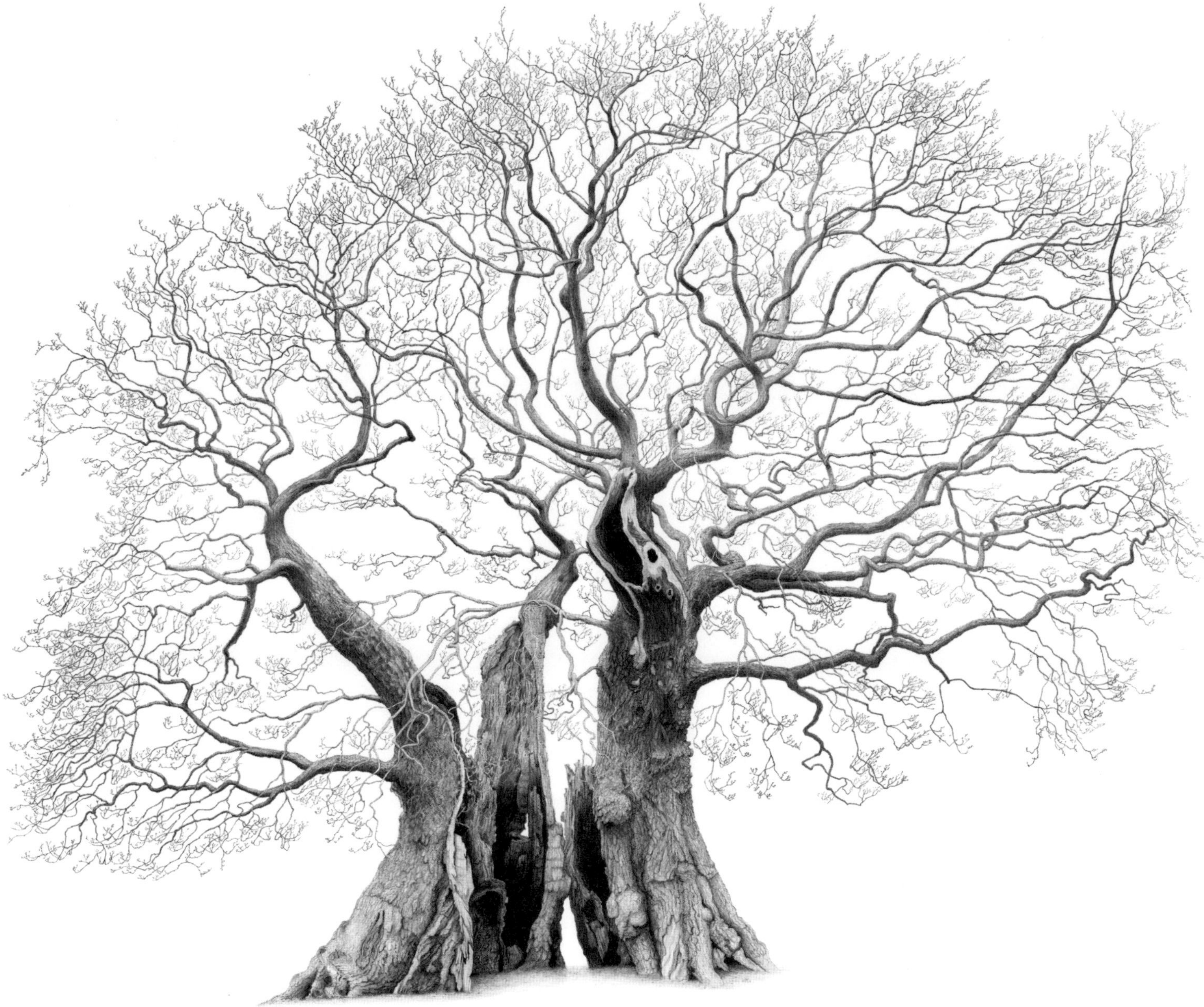

The tree which moves some to tears of joy is in the eyes of others only a green thing that stands in the way. Some see nature all ridicule and deformity ... and some scarce see nature at all. But to the eyes of the man of imagination, nature is imagination itself.

William Blake
Letter to the Reverend John Trusler, 1777

The Marton Oak
Detail

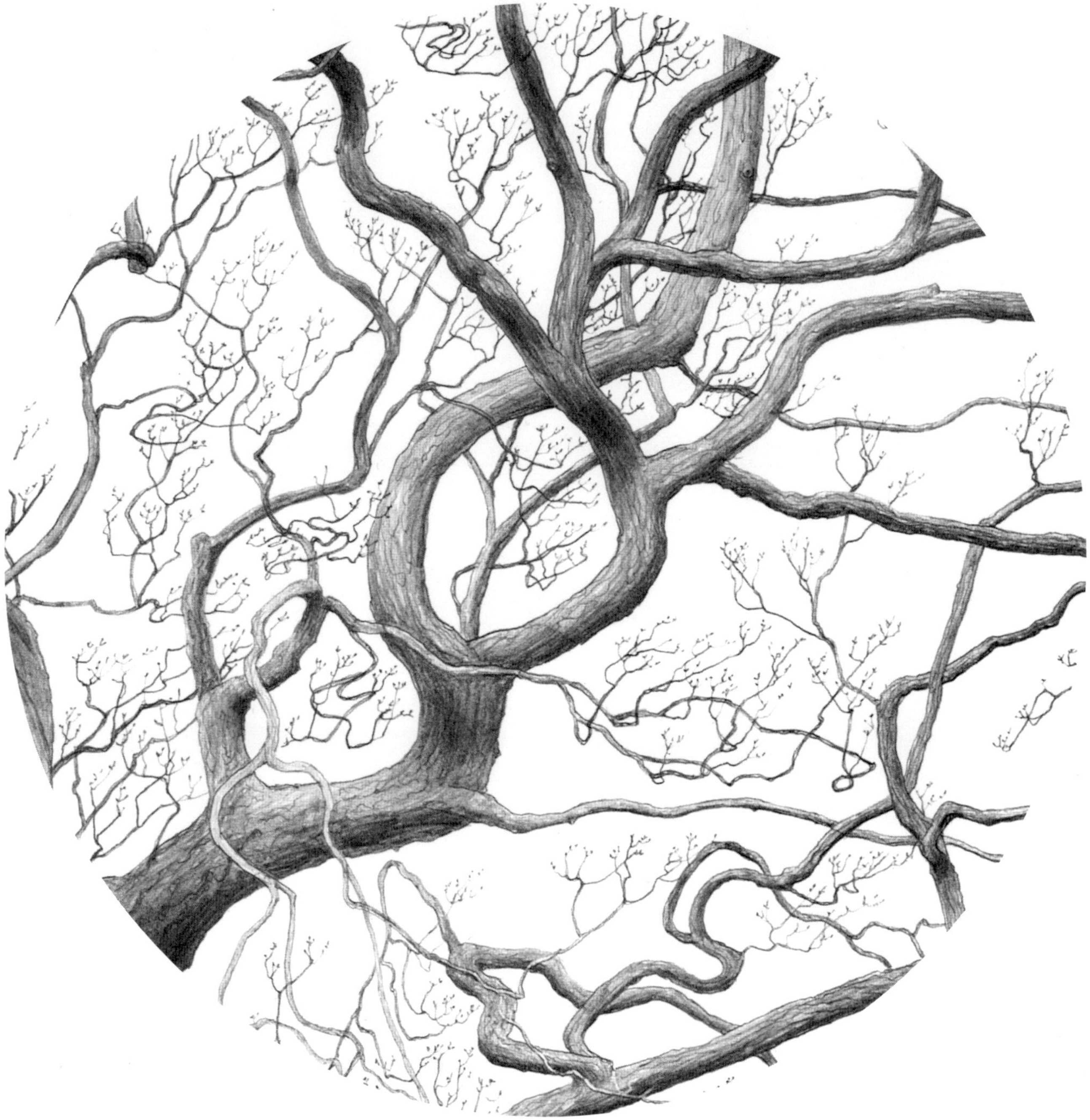

The Bowthorpe Oak
Lincolnshire
Quercus robur
Graphite on paper
150 × 120 cm
2011

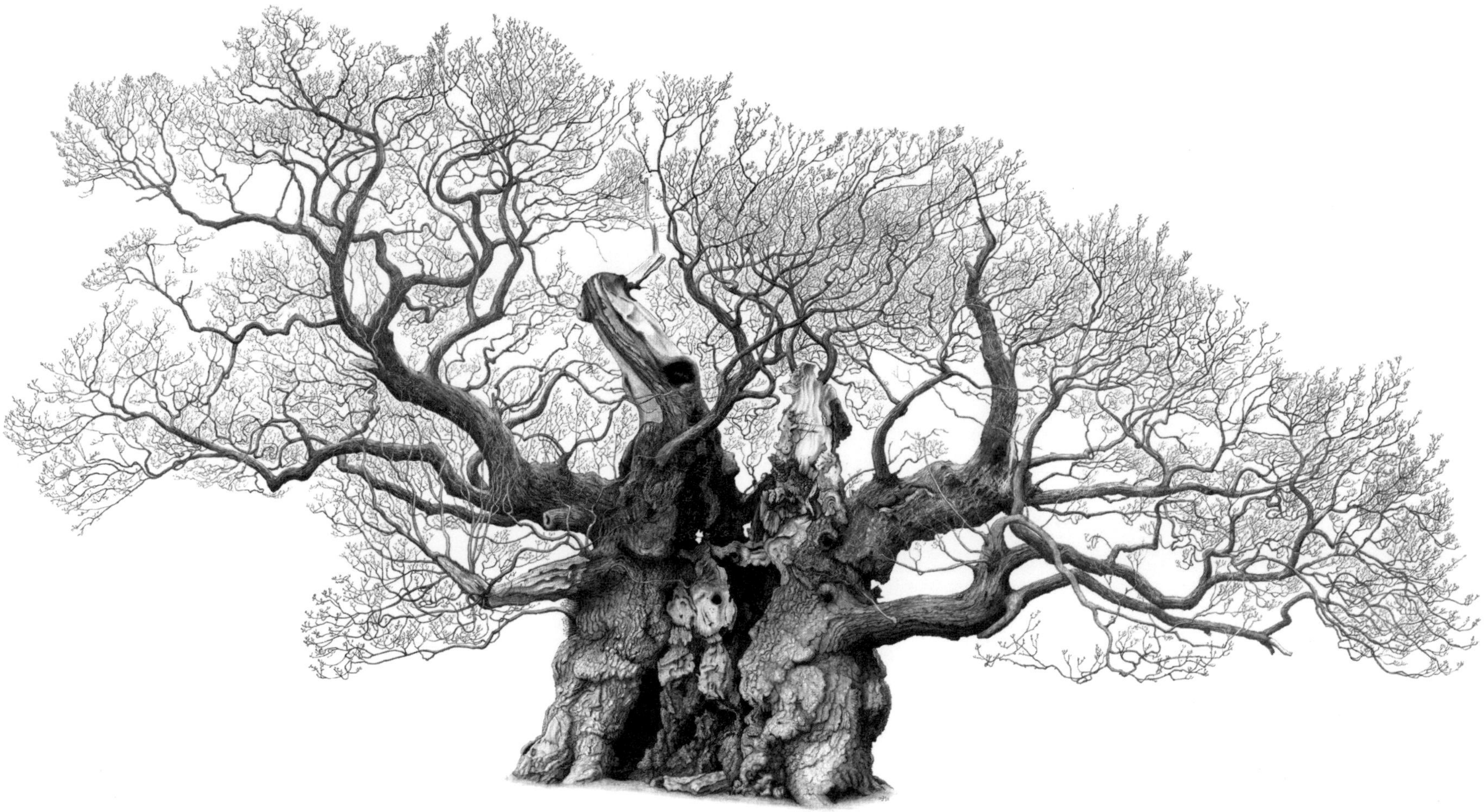

To such an extent does nature delight and abound in variety that among her trees there is not one plant to be found which is exactly like another; and not only among the plants, but among the boughs, the leaves and the fruits, you will not find one which is exactly similar to another.

Leonardo da Vinci
Notebooks

The Bowthorpe Oak
Detail

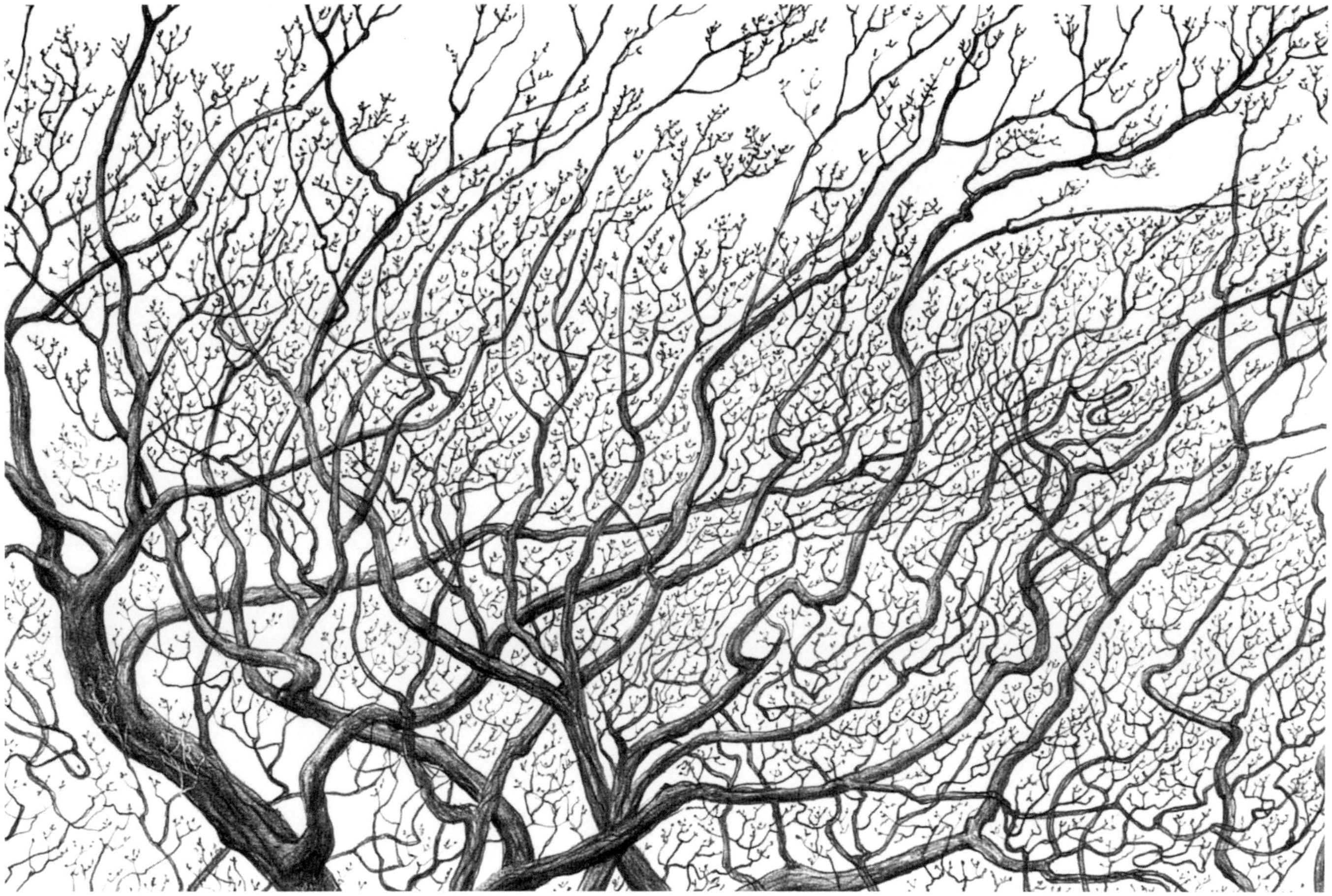

The King John Oak
Devon
Quercus robur
Graphite on paper
150 × 120 cm
2014

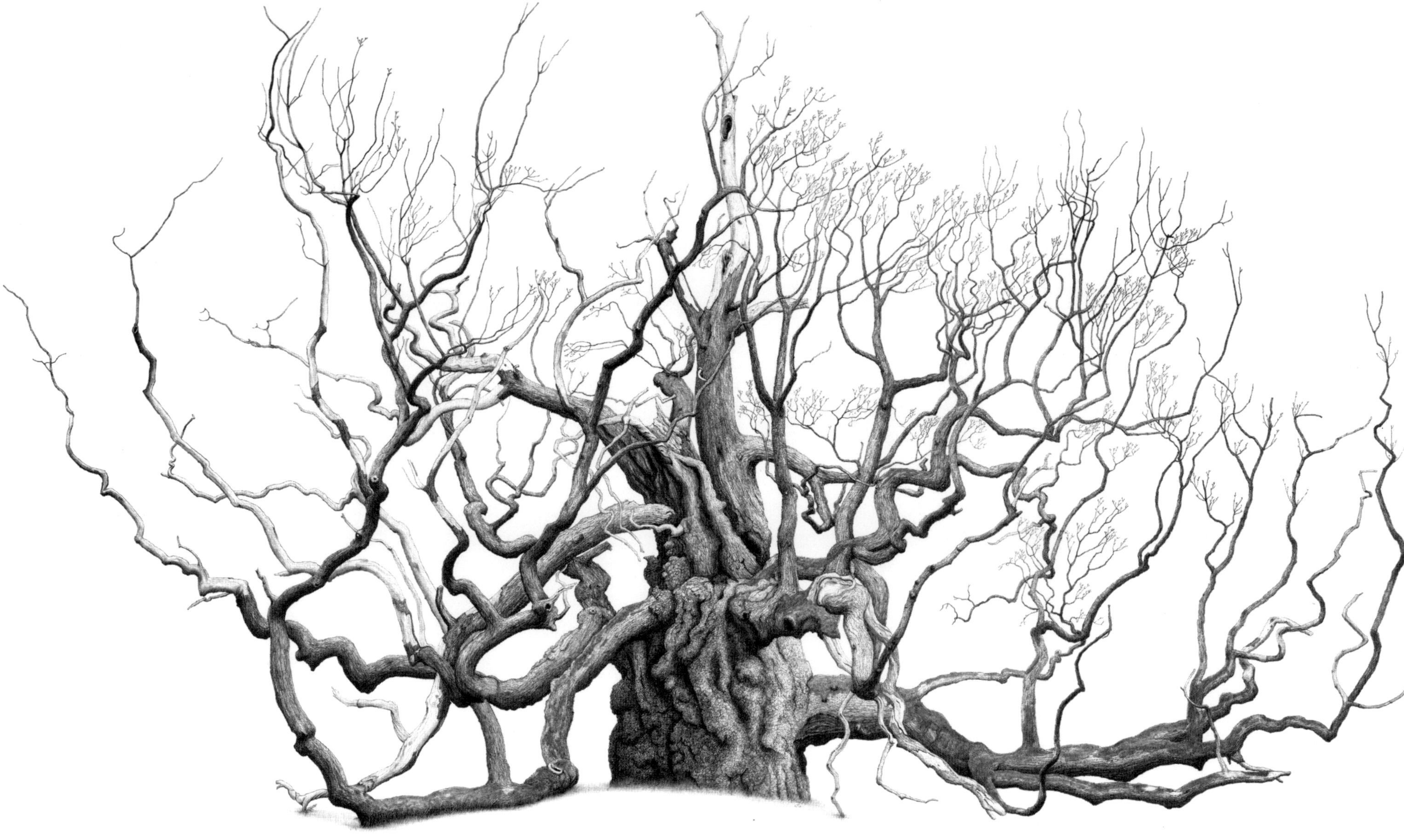

The King John Oak
Detail

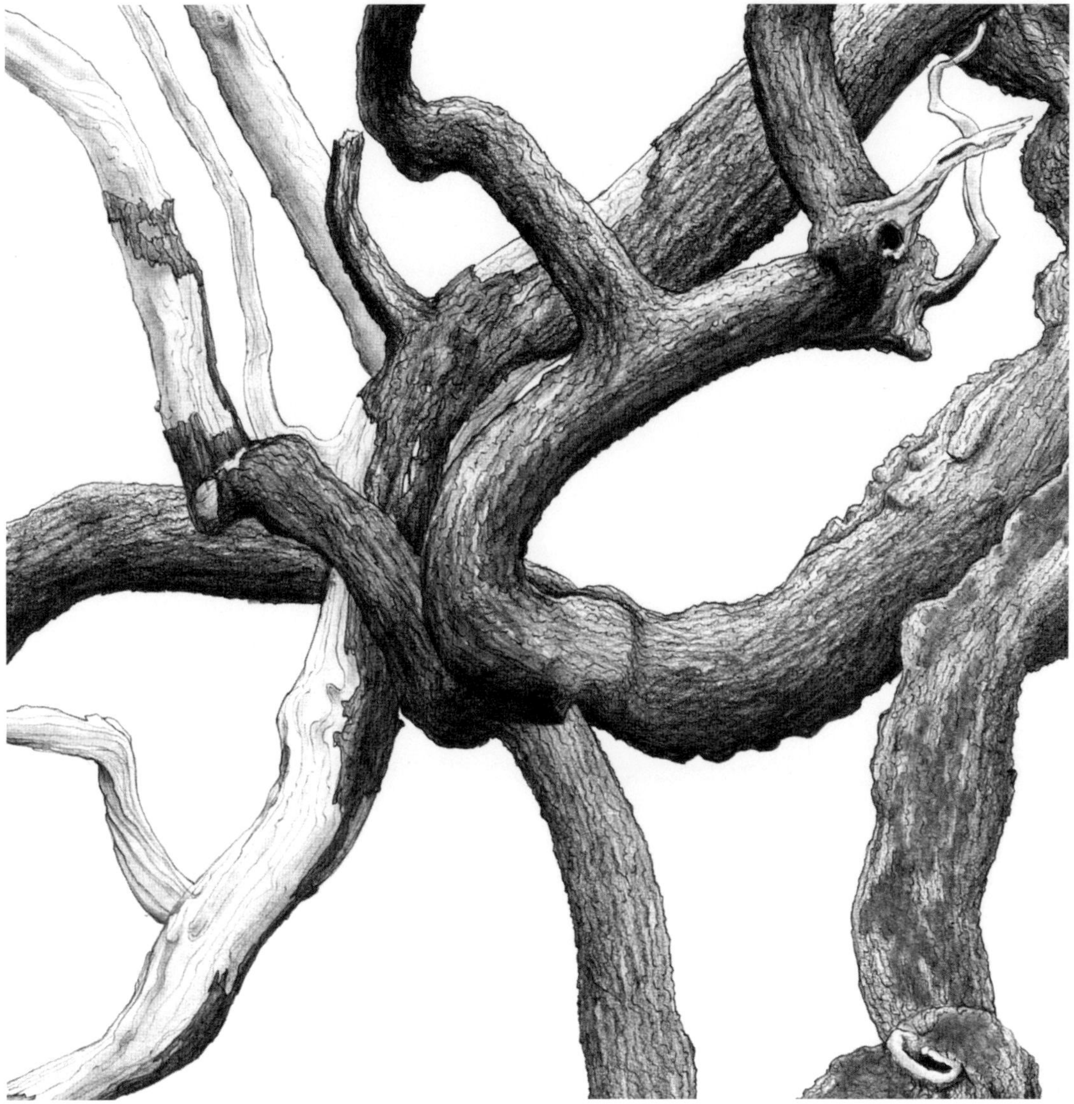

The Old Man of Calke
Derbyshire
Quercus robur
Graphite on paper
150 × 120 cm
2012

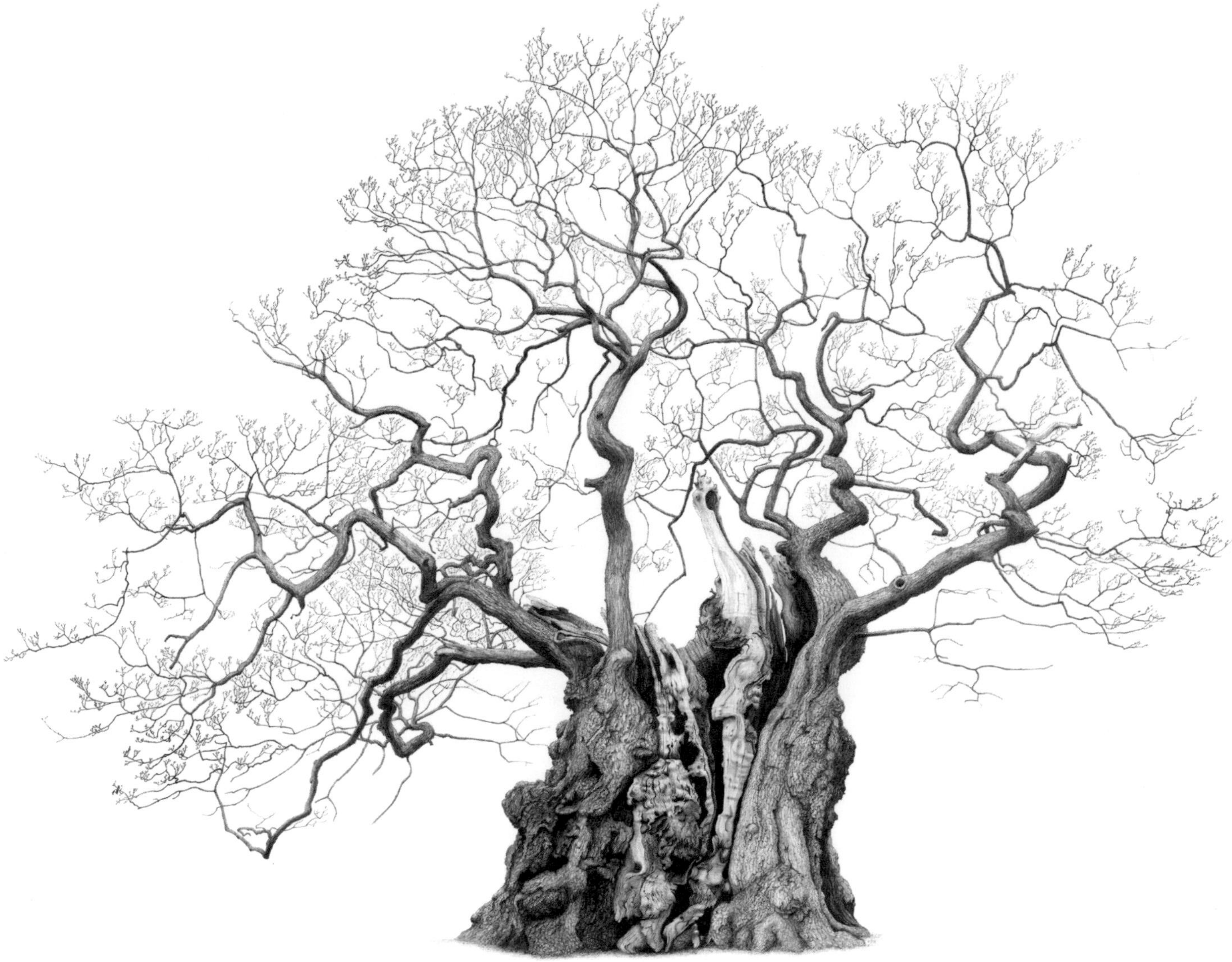

We have nothing to fear and a great deal to learn from trees, that vigorous and pacific tribe which without stint produces strengthening essences for us, soothing balms, and in whose gracious company we spend so many cool, silent, and intimate hours.

Marcel Proust
Regrets, Reveries, Changing Skies

The Old Man of Calke
Detail

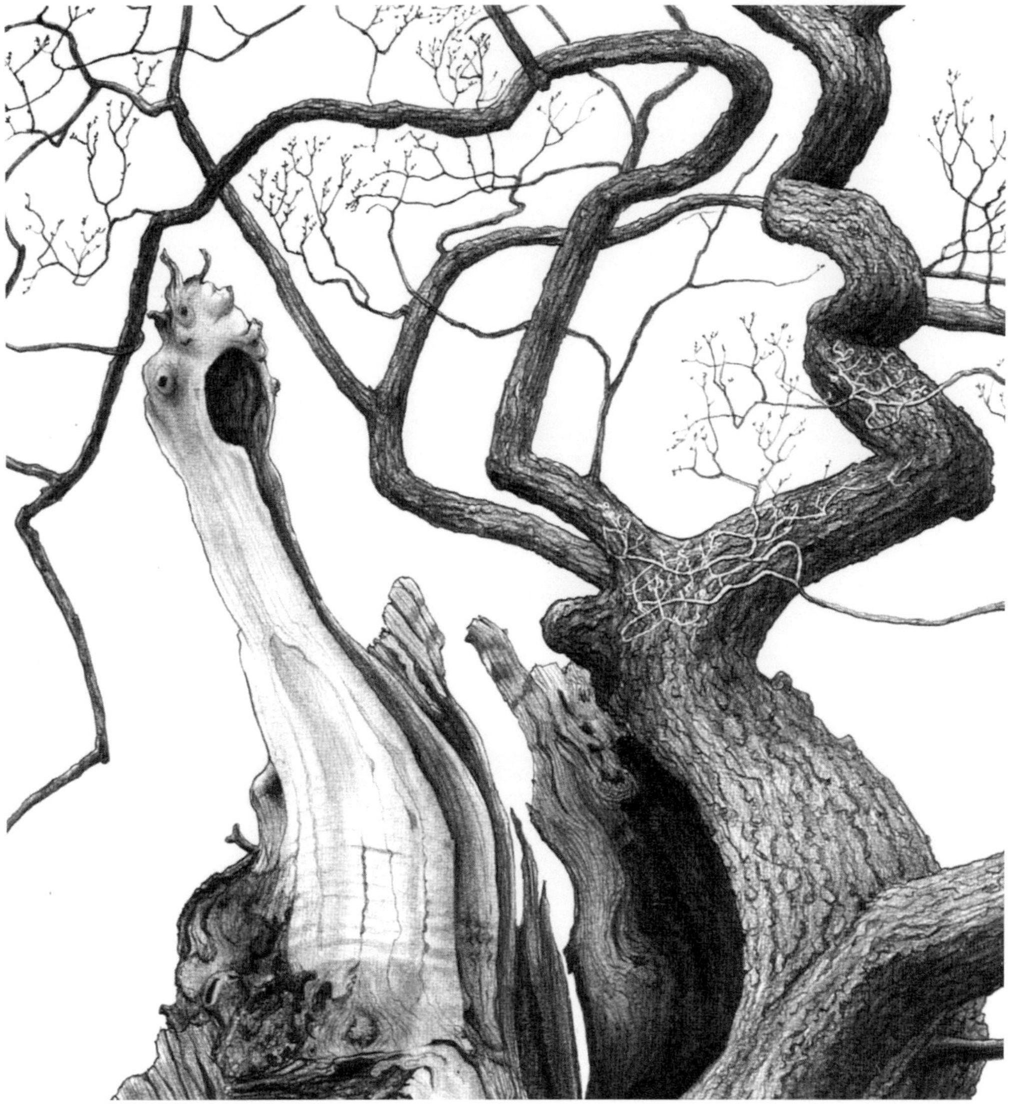

Billy Wilkins
Dorset
Quercus robur
Graphite on paper
150 × 120 cm
2013

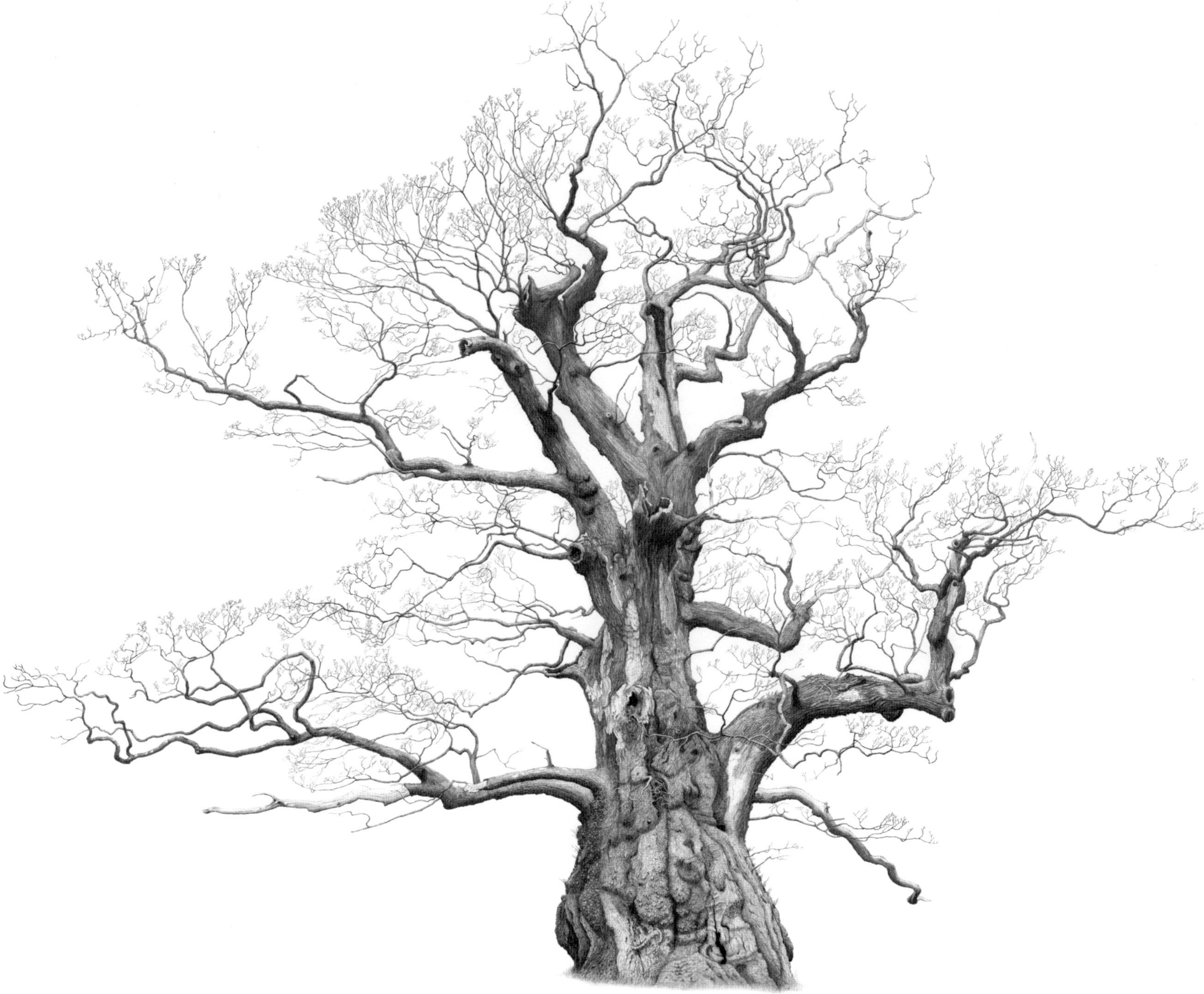

All his leaves,
Fall'n at length,
Look he stands,
Trunk and bough,
Naked strength.

Alfred Lord Tennyson
The Foresters

Billy Wilkins
Detail

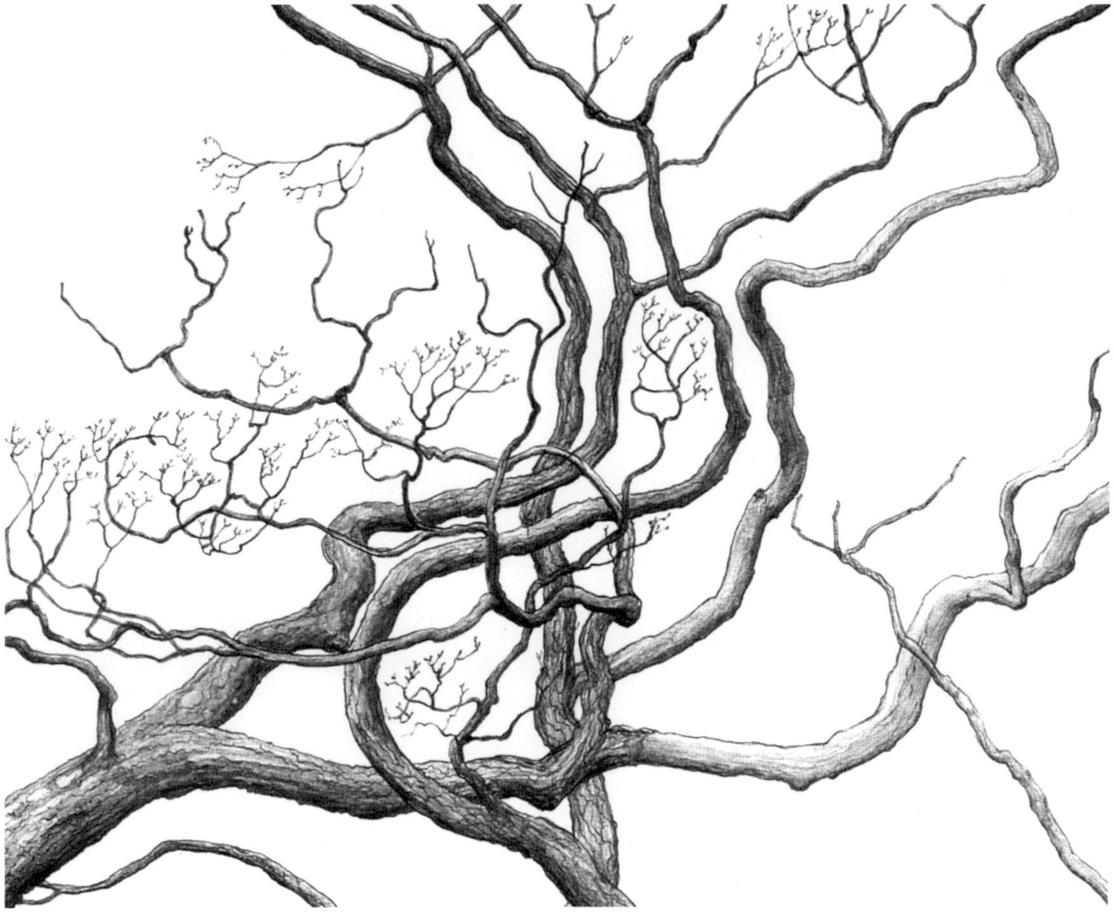

The Queen Elizabeth I Oak
Sussex
Quercus petraea
Graphite on paper
150 × 120 cm
2014

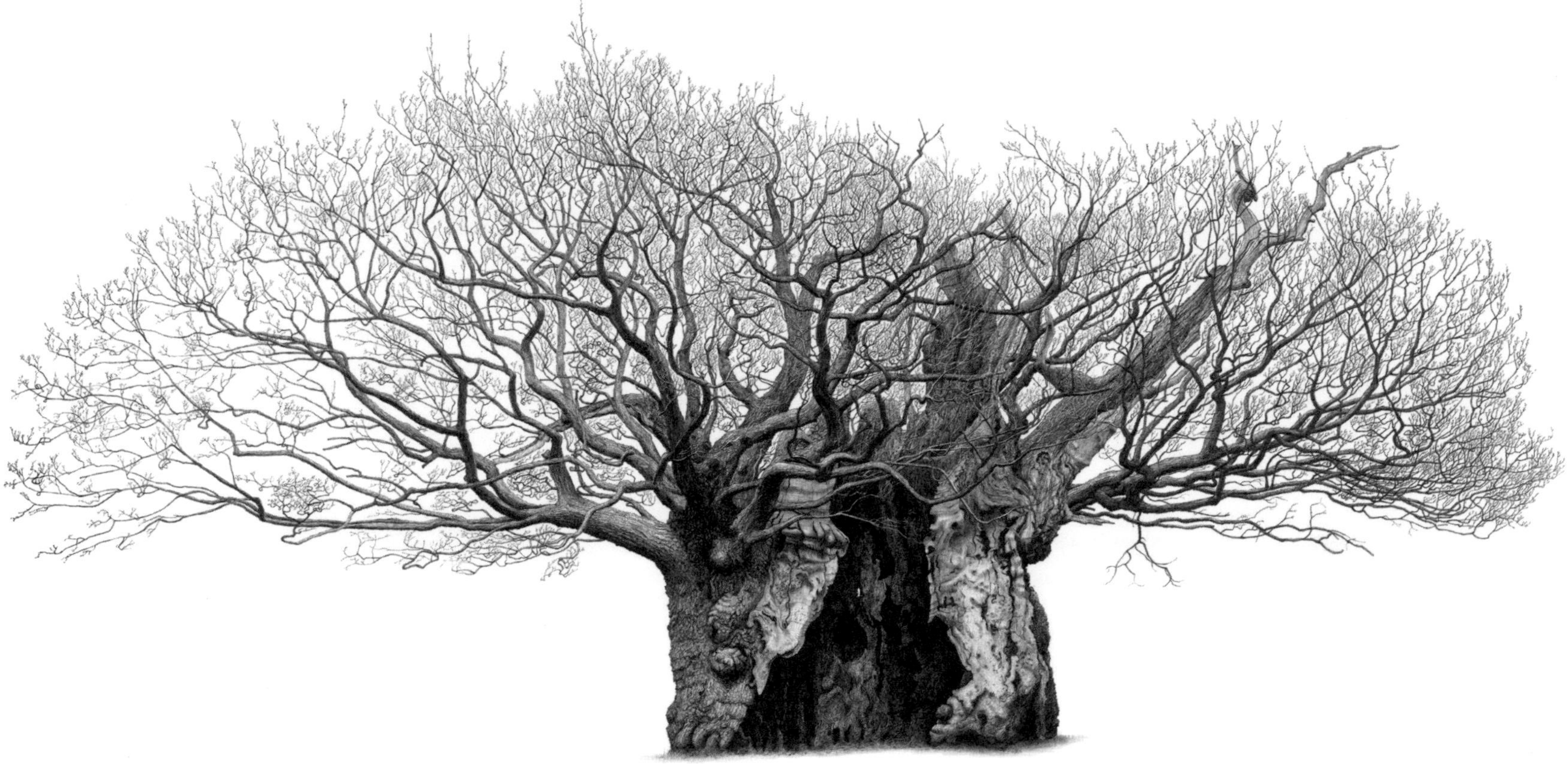

The Queen Elizabeth I Oak
Detail

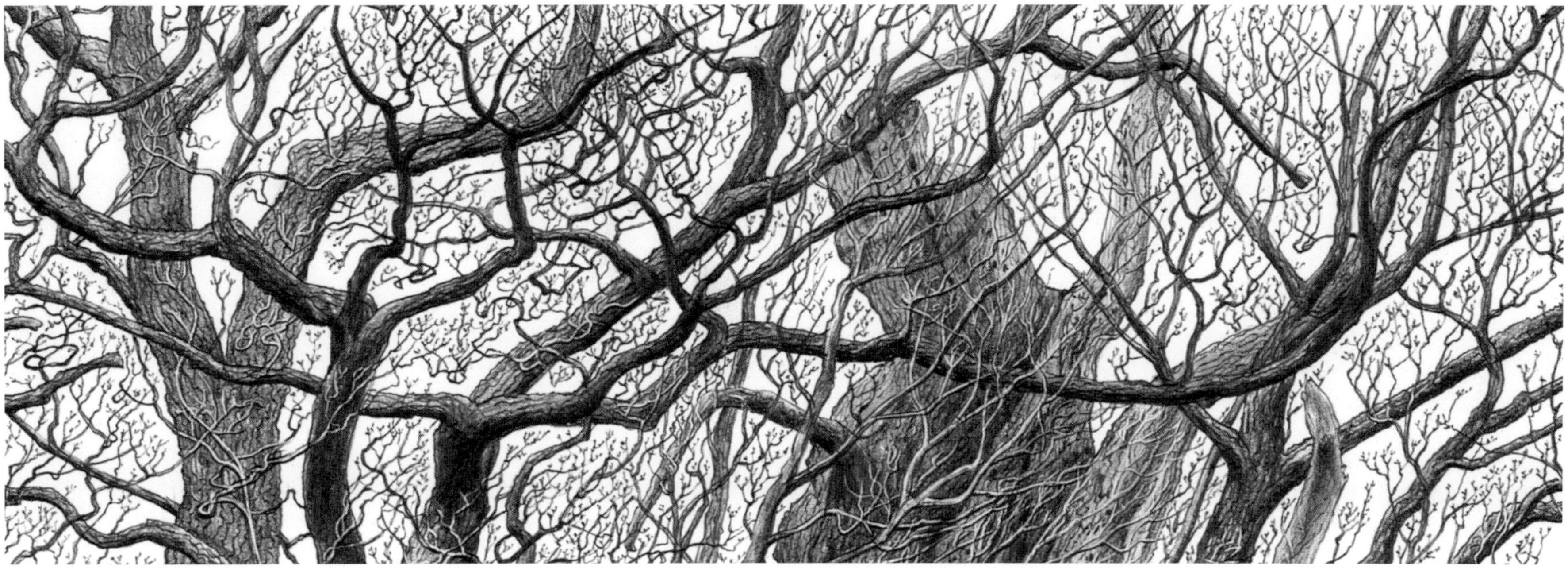

The Gospel Oak
Herefordshire
Quercus robur
Graphite on paper
150 × 120 cm
2012

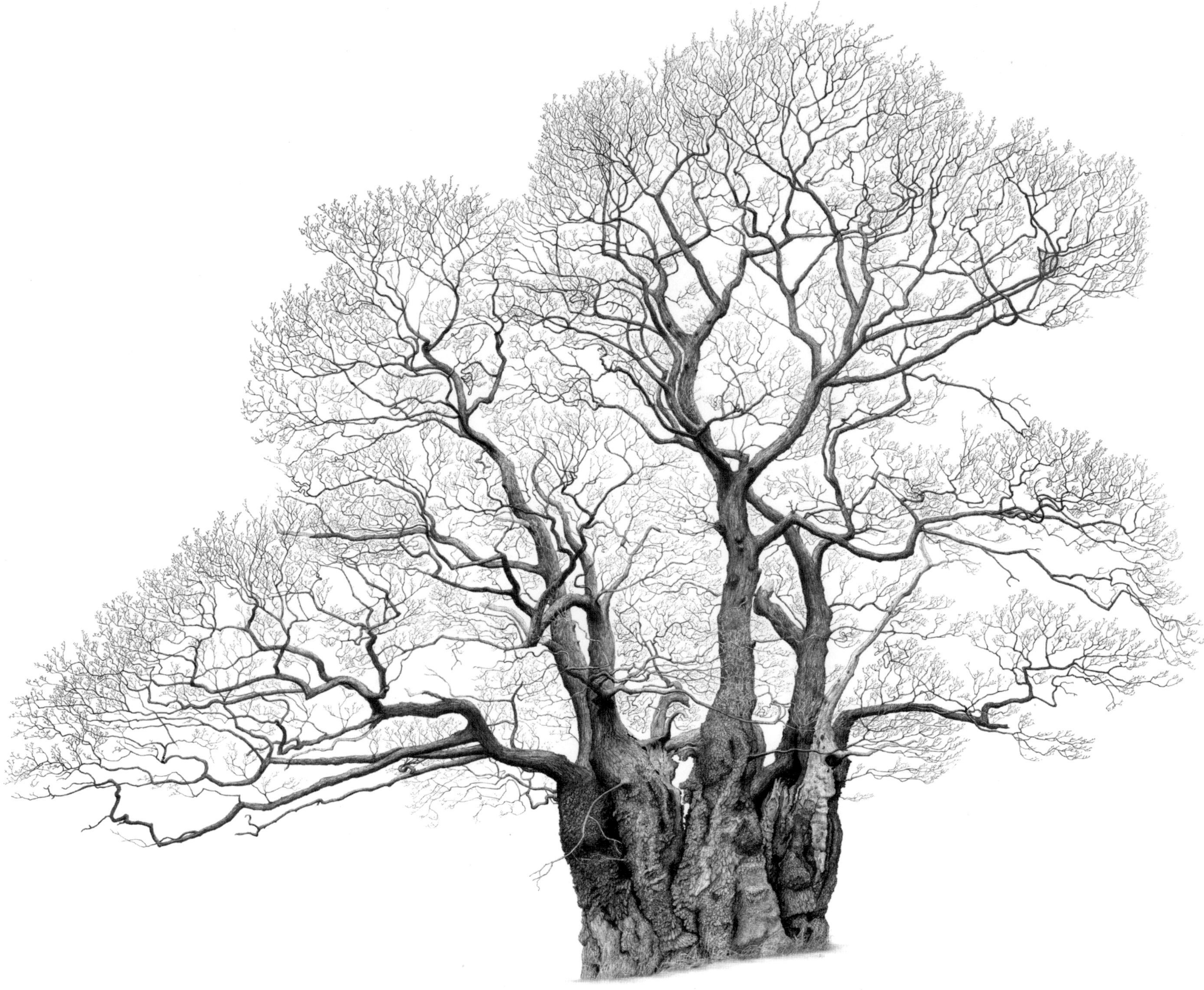

Time made thee what thou wast, king of the woods.
And Time hath made thee what thou art ...
First a seedling hid in grass,
Then twig, then sapling, and, as century rolled
Slow after century, a giant bulk
Of girth enormous with moss-cushioned root
Upheaved above the soil, and sides embossed
With prominent wens globose, till at the last
The rottenness which Time is charged to inflict
On other mighty ones found also thee.

William Cowper
Yardley Oak

The Gospel Oak
Detail

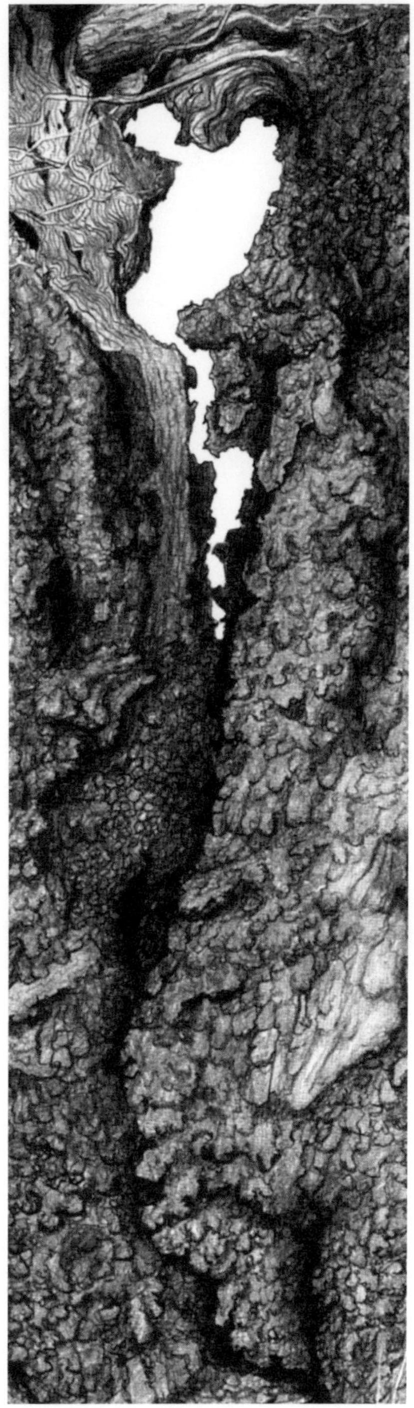

The Mottisfont or Oakley Oak
Dorset
Quercus robur
Graphite on paper
150 × 120 cm
2013

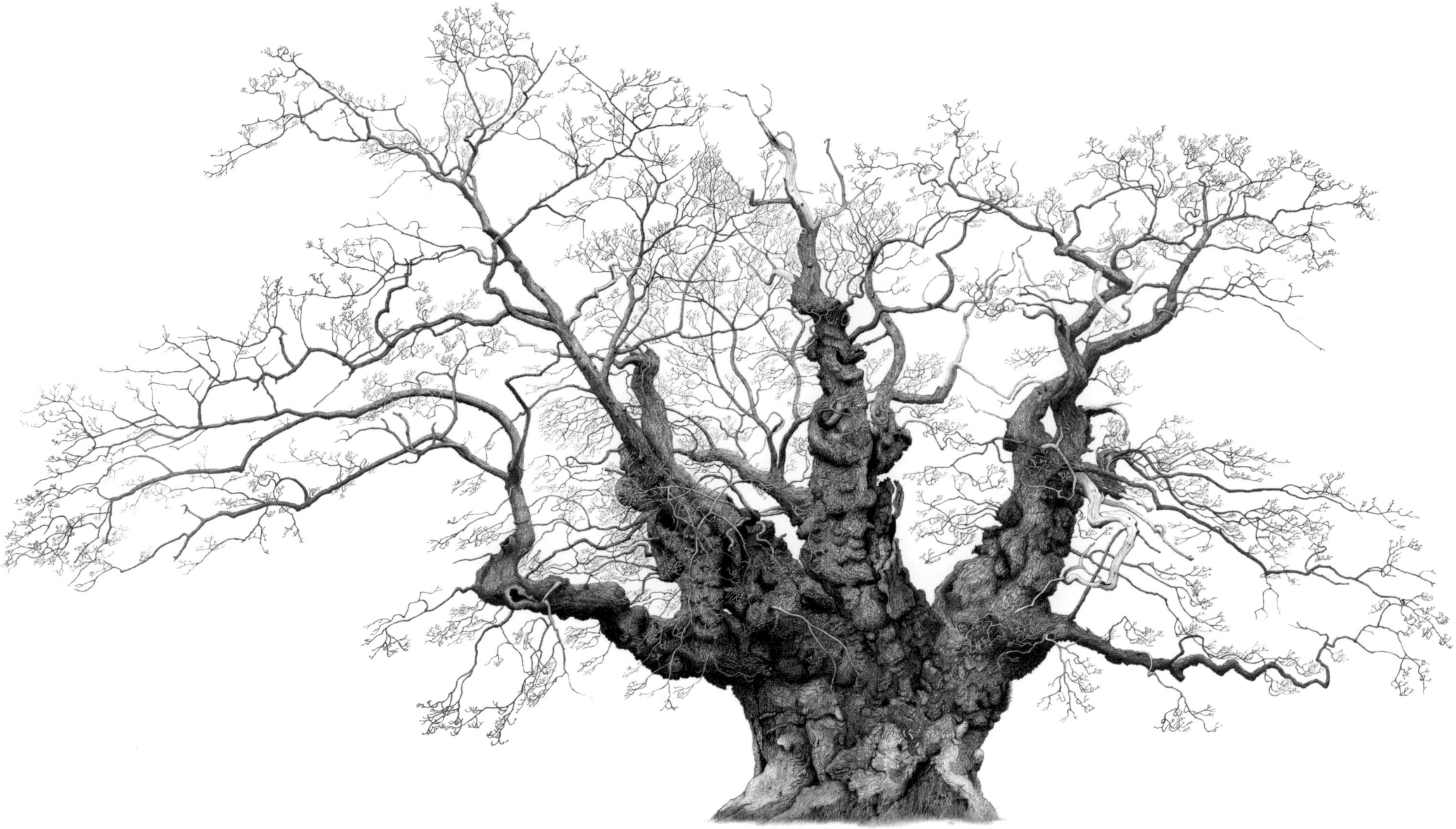

The Mottisfont or Oakley Oak
Detail

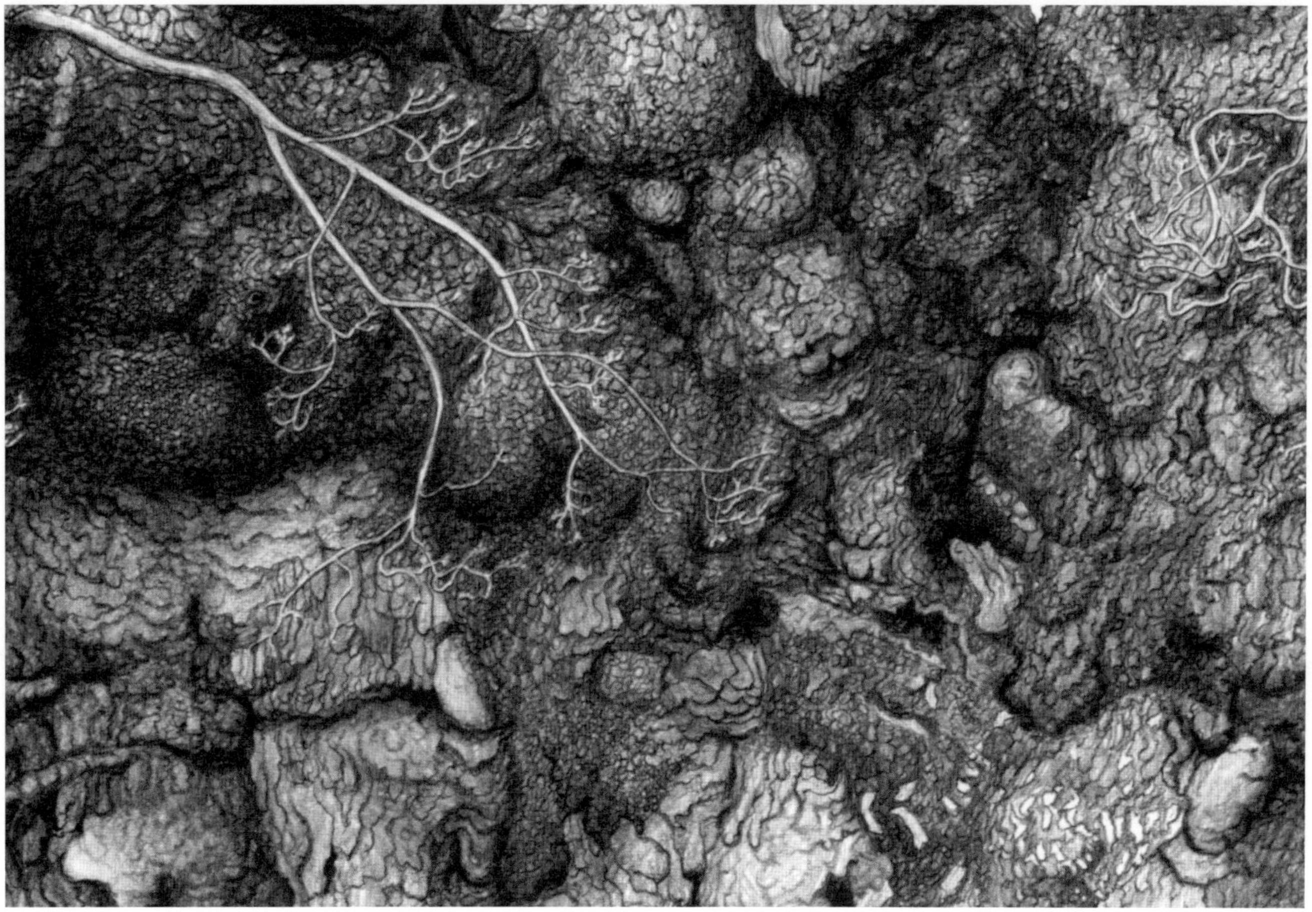

The Major Oak
Nottinghamshire
Quercus robur
Graphite on paper
150 × 120 cm
2012

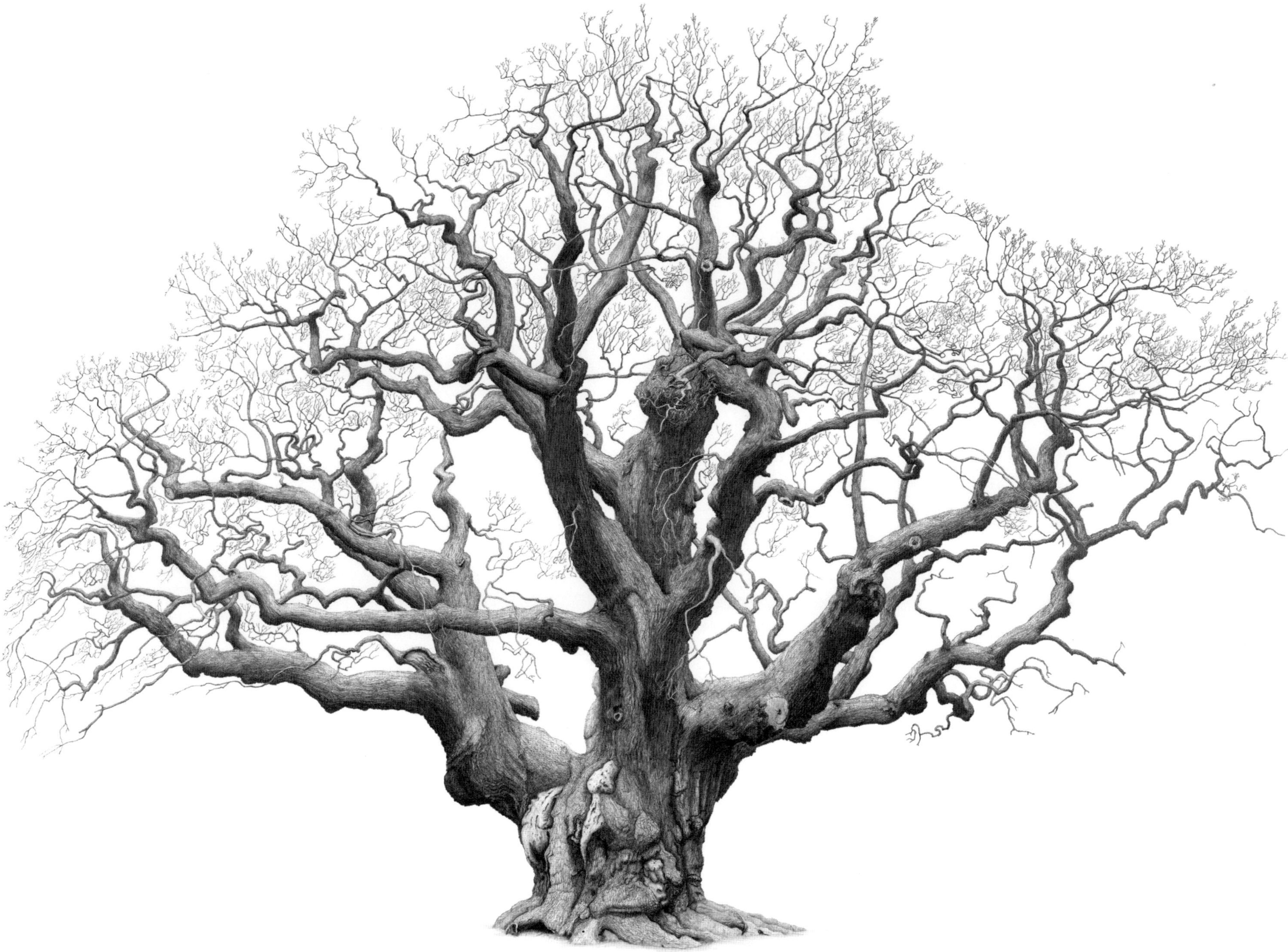

The Major Oak
Detail

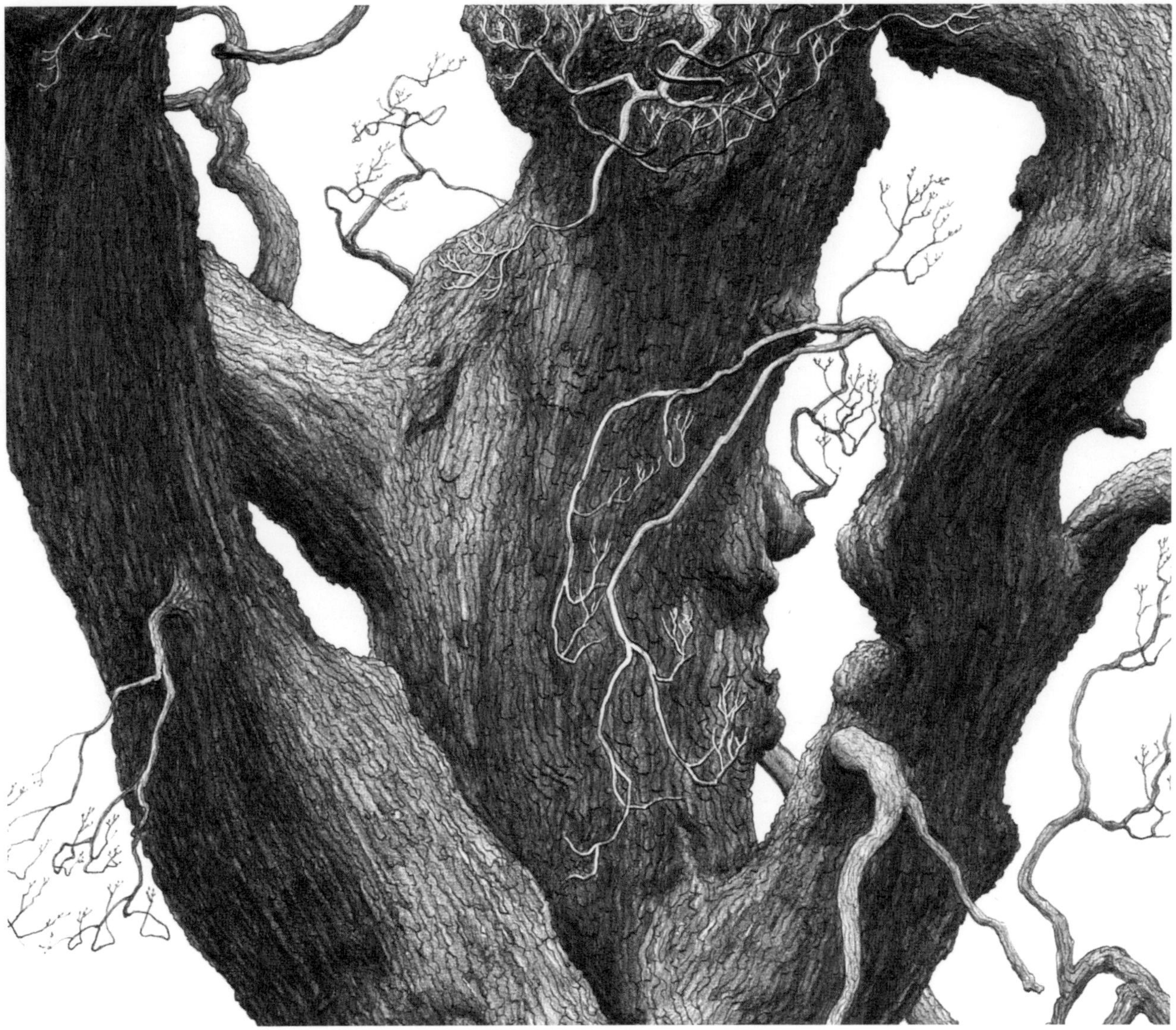

Judge Wyndham's Oak
Dorset
Quercus robur
Graphite on paper
150 × 120 cm
2011

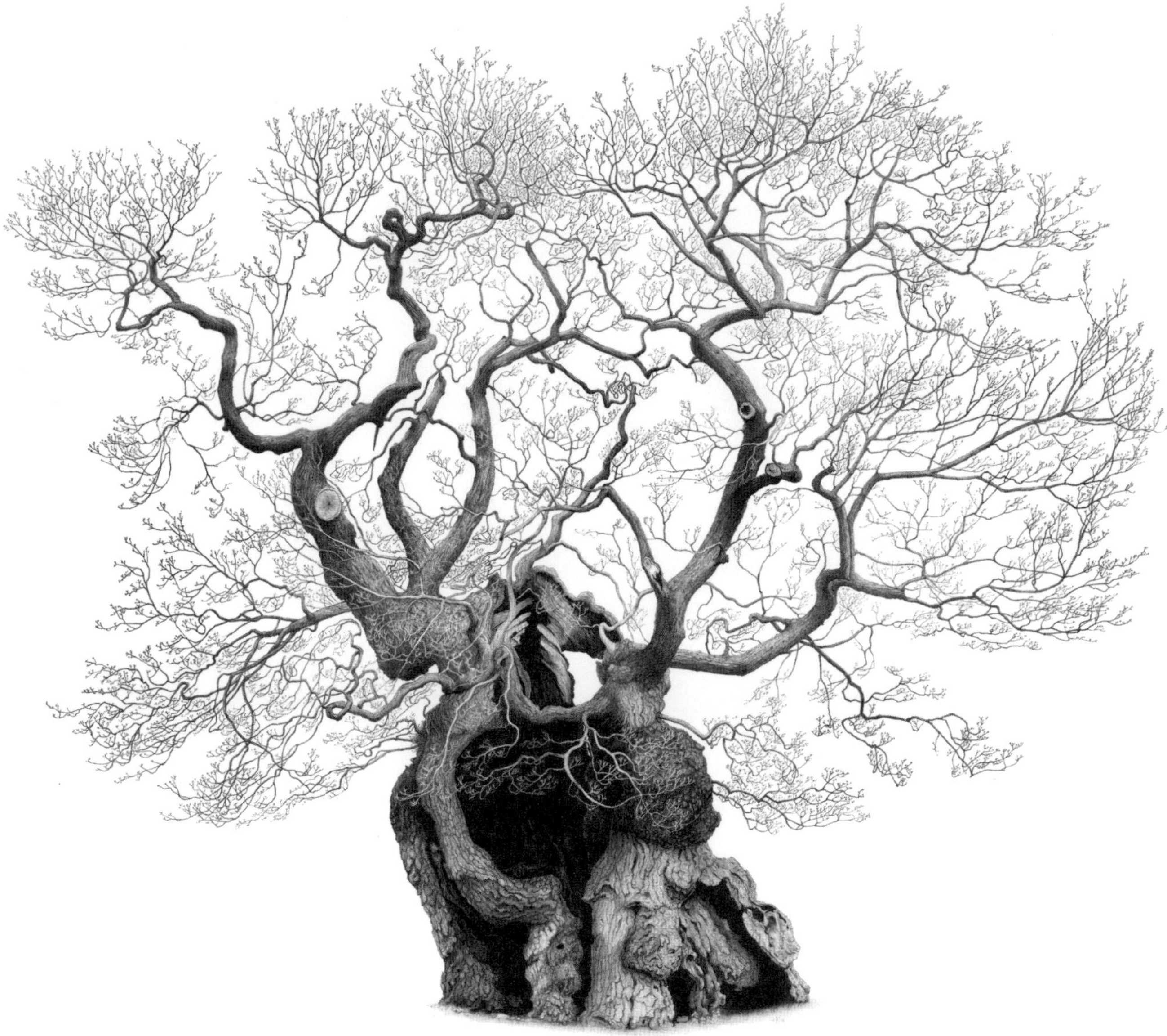

A tree, young or old, if admired, remains a definite vision, and when after long absence it is visited again, the meeting place is approached with feelings of pleasure and curiosity as to how one's friend had fared, even with thoughts as to what changes may come to tree or visitor since first they met.

Charles Eley
Gardening for the Twentieth Century

Judge Wyndham's Oak
Detail

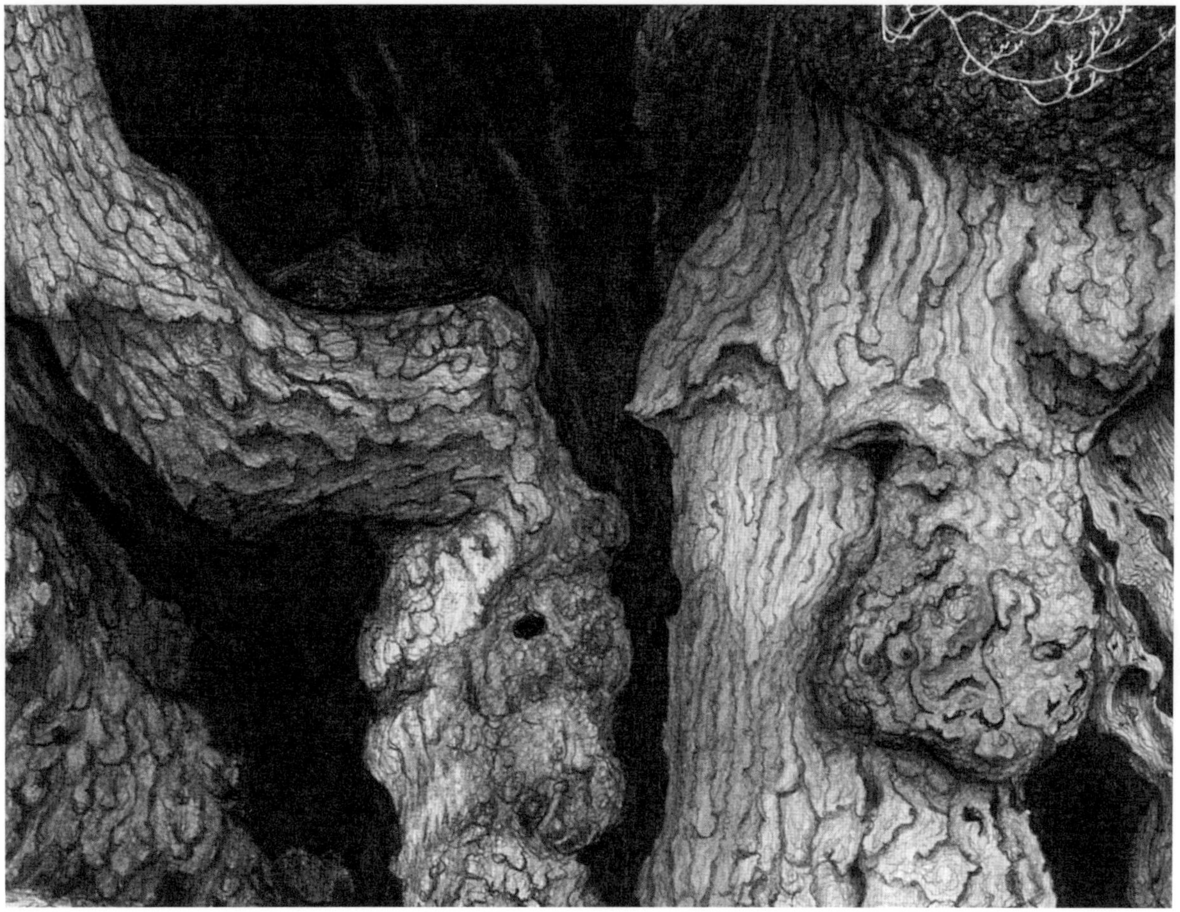

The Chaceley Oak
Gloucestershire
Quercus robur
Graphite on paper
150 × 120 cm
2011

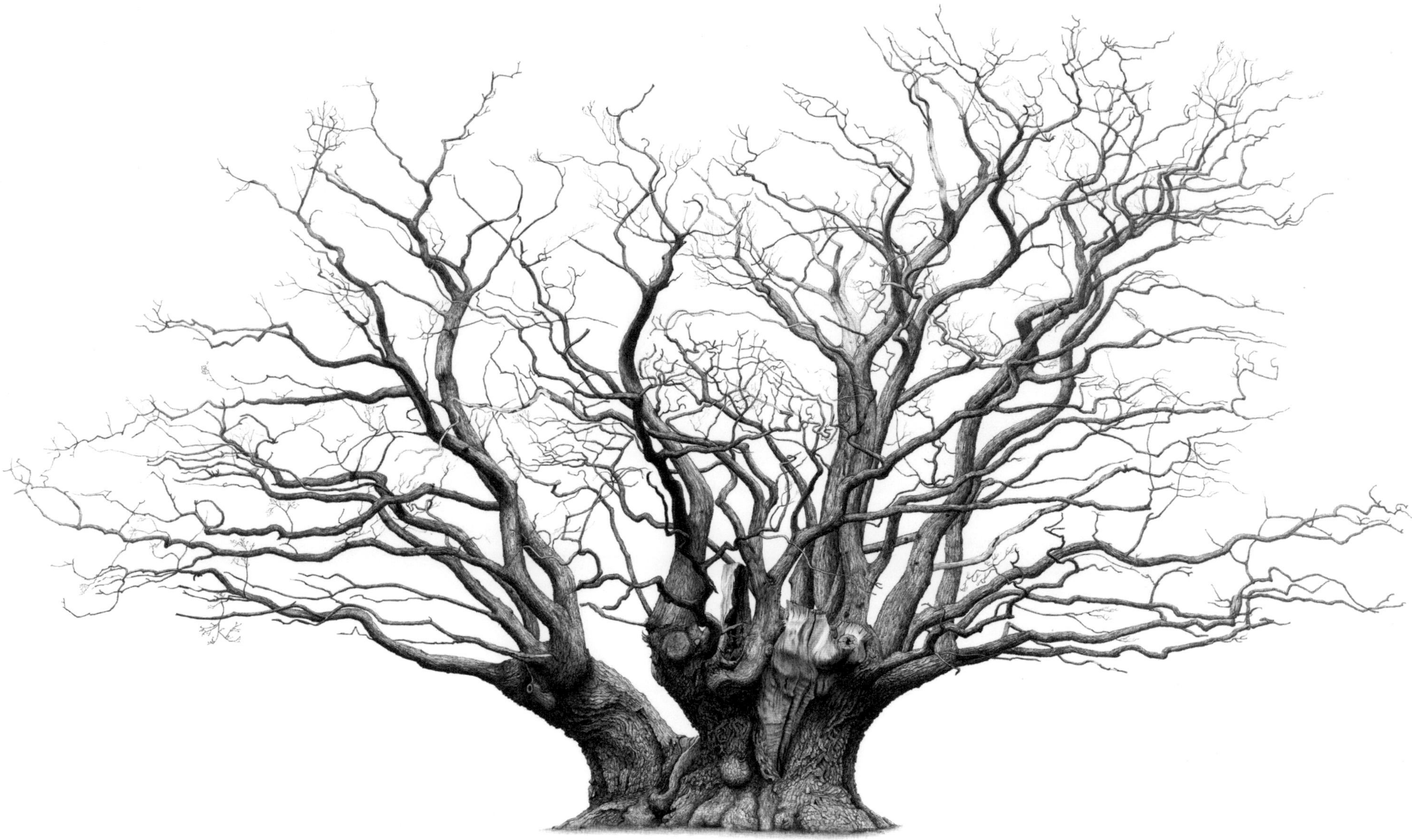

The Chaceley Oak
Detail

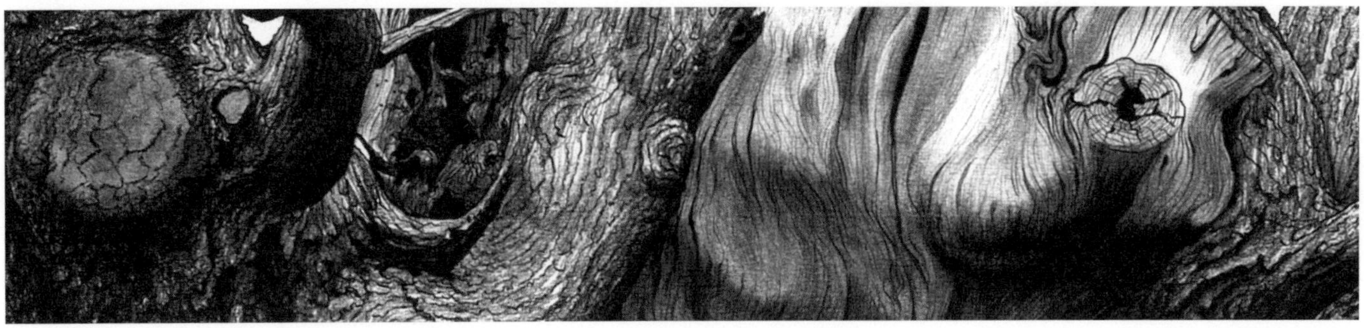

The Pontfadog Oak
Wrexham
Quercus petraea
Graphite on paper
150 × 120 cm
2013

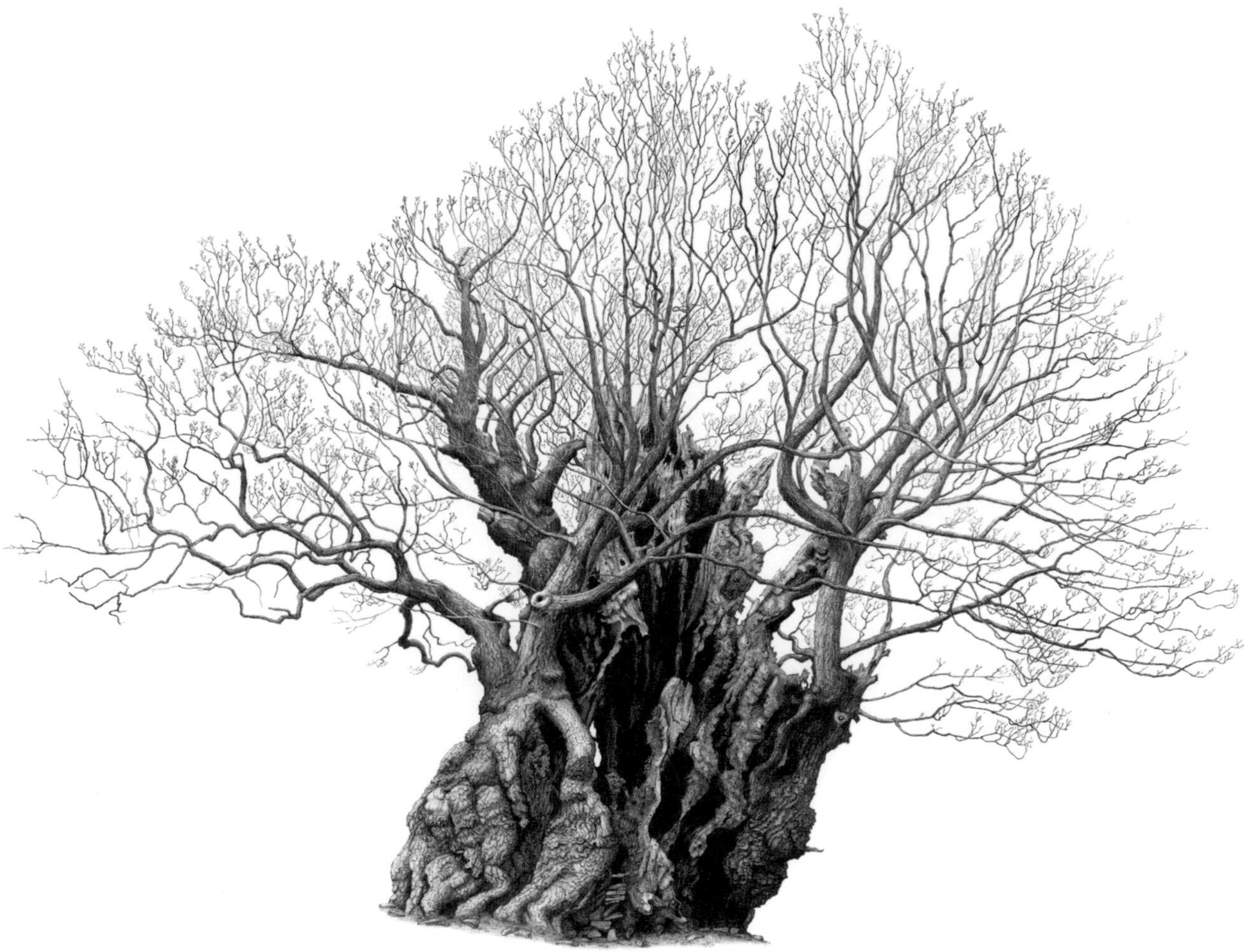

There grew an aged tree on the green ...
A goodly Oak sometime had it been.
With arms fall strong and largely displayed,
But of their leaves they were disarrayed:
The body big, and mightily weight,
Throughly rooted, and of wondrous height;
Whilom had been the king of the field,
And mochell mast to th' husband did yield,
And with his nuts larded many swine:
But now the grey moss marred his rine;
His bared boughs were beaten with storms,
His top was bald and wasted with worms,
His honour decayed, his branches sere.

Edmund Spenser
The Shepheardes Calender

The Pontfadog Oak
Detail

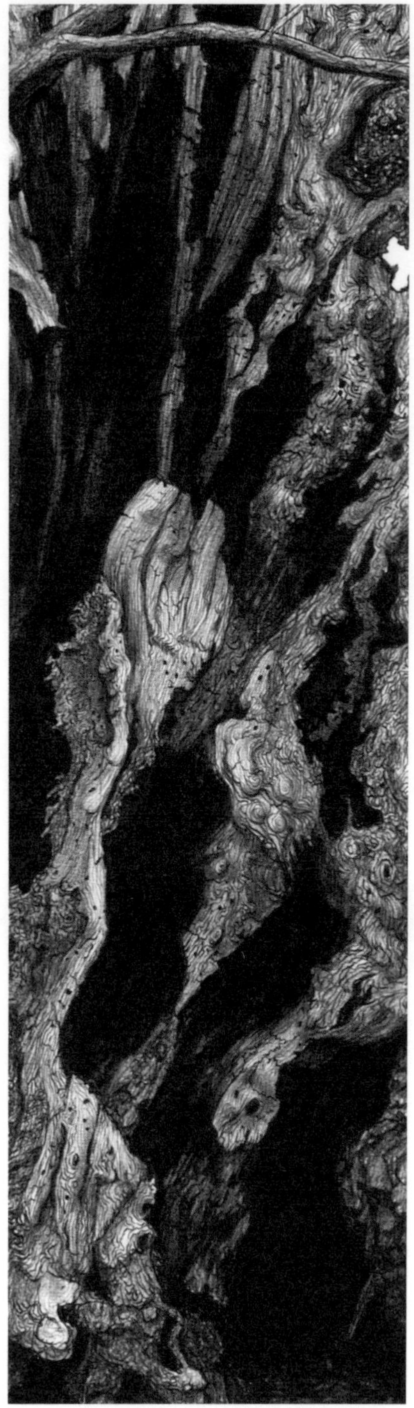

The Capon Oak
Scottish Borders
Quercus petraea
Graphite on paper
150 × 120 cm
2014

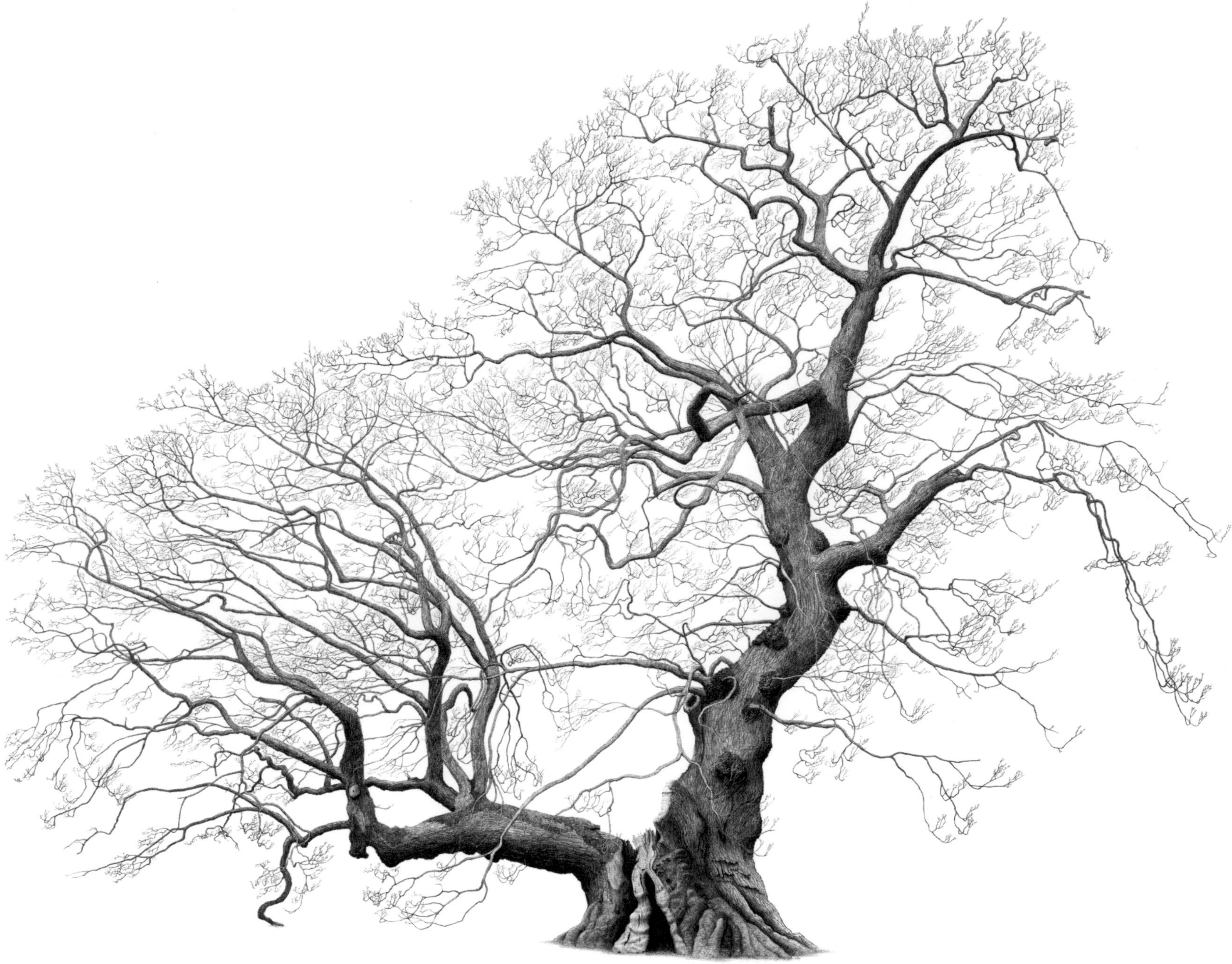

The Capon Oak
Detail

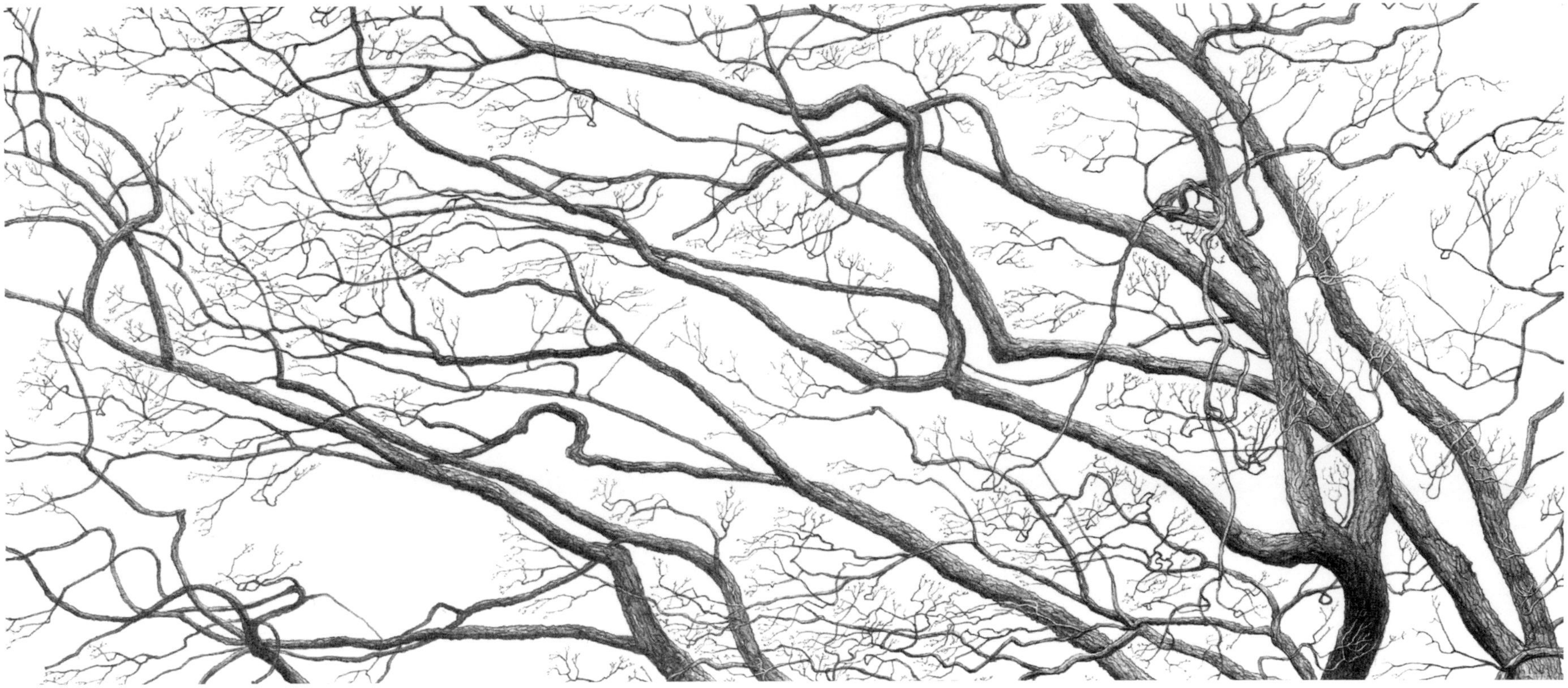

The Eastcourt Oak
Gloucestershire
Quercus robur
Graphite on paper
150 × 120 cm
2011

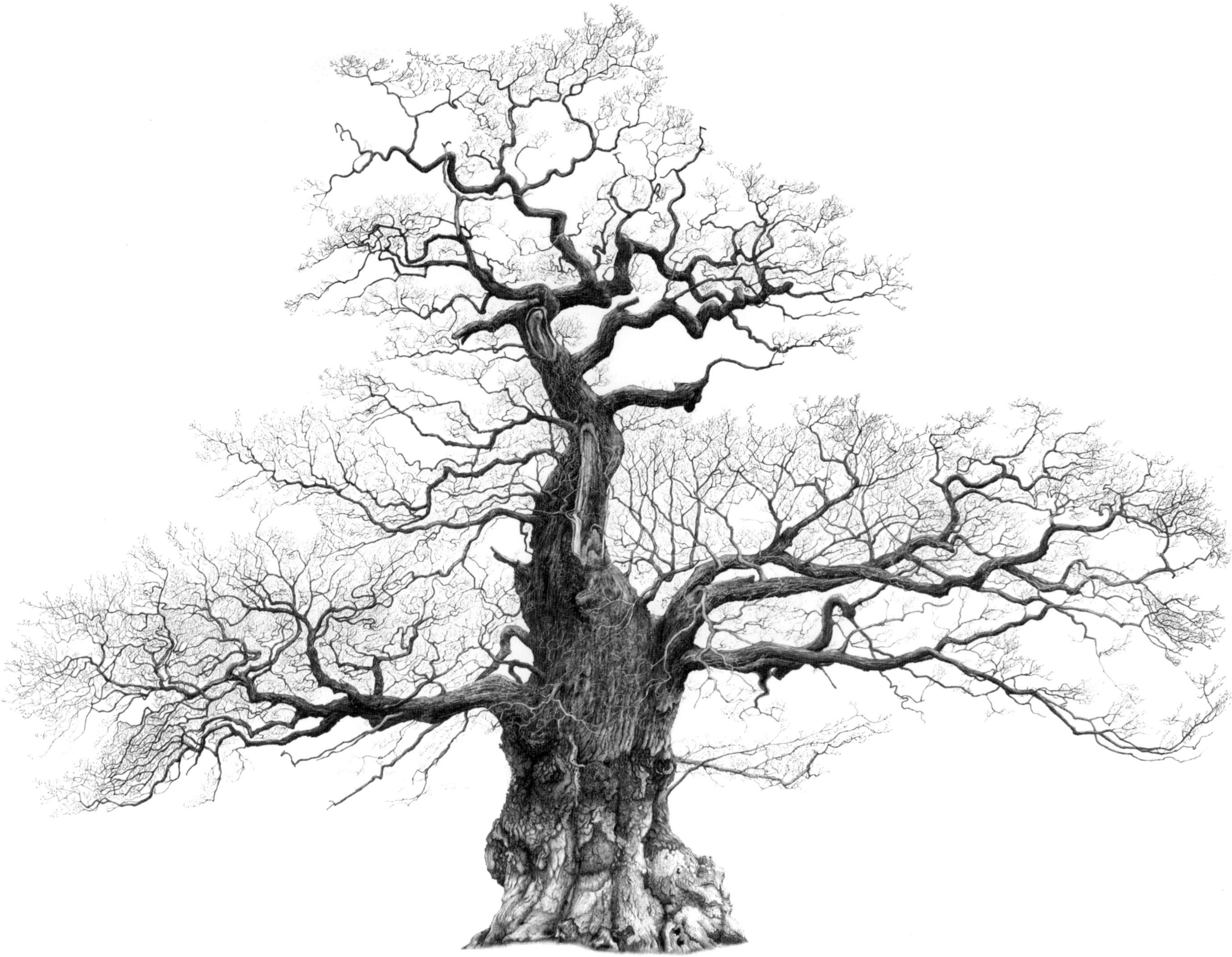

And there was no sound in the cavern of foliage except one call of a cuckoo as I entered and the warbling of a blackbird that mused in the oaks then laughed and was silent and mused again and filled the mind with the fairest images of solitude.

Edward Thomas
The South Country

The Eastcourt Oak
Detail

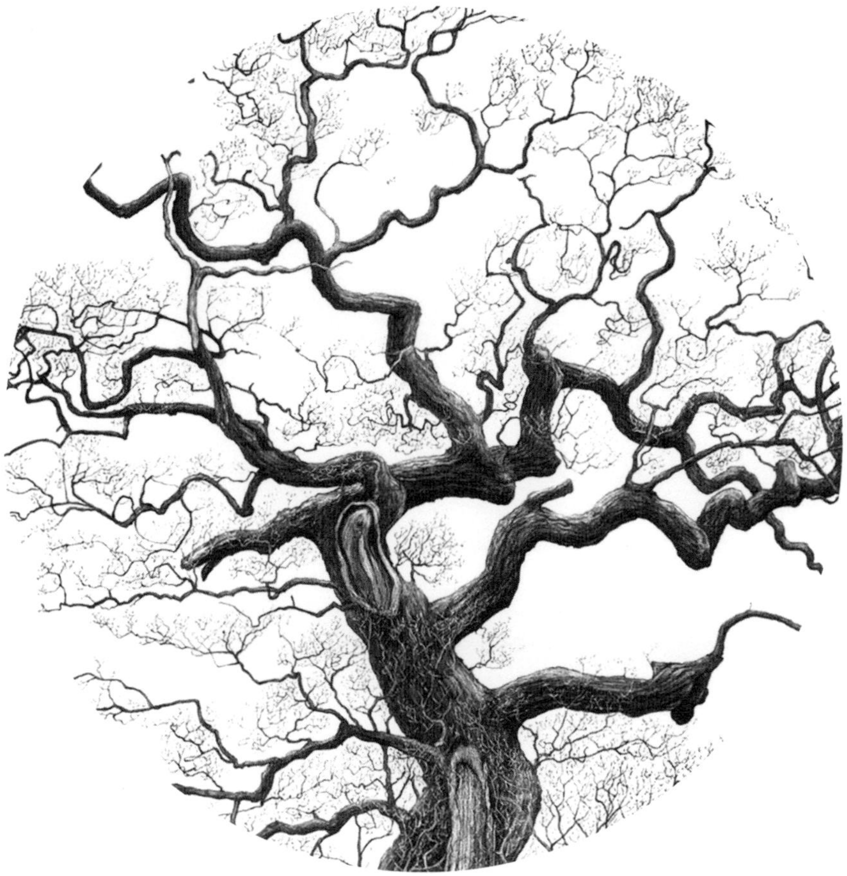

The Darley Oak
Cornwall
Quercus robur
Graphite on paper
150 × 120 cm
2011

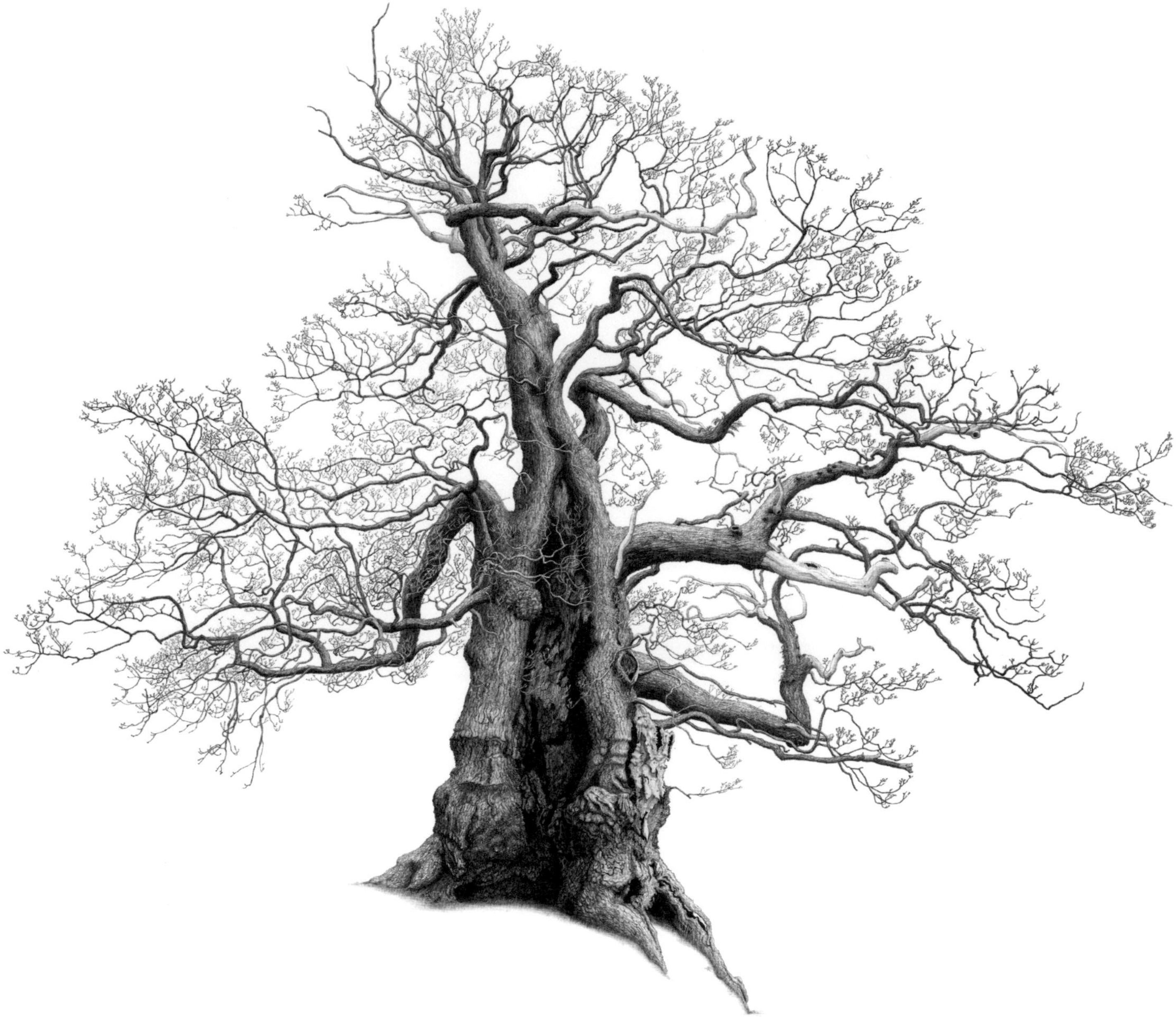

The Darley Oak
Detail

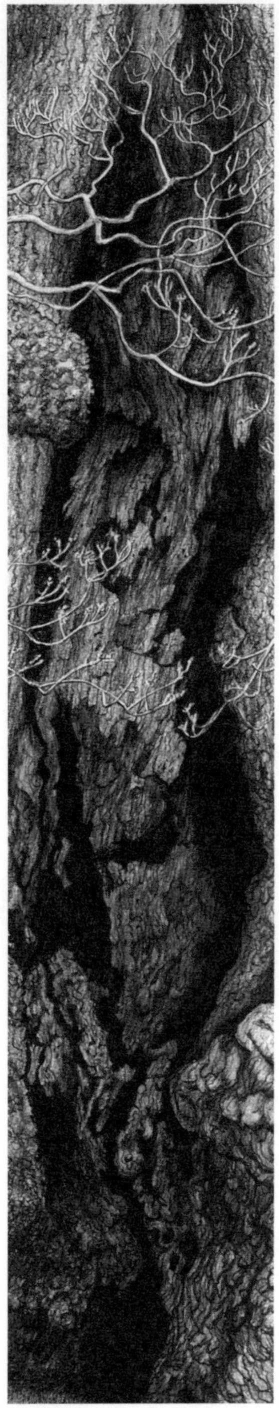

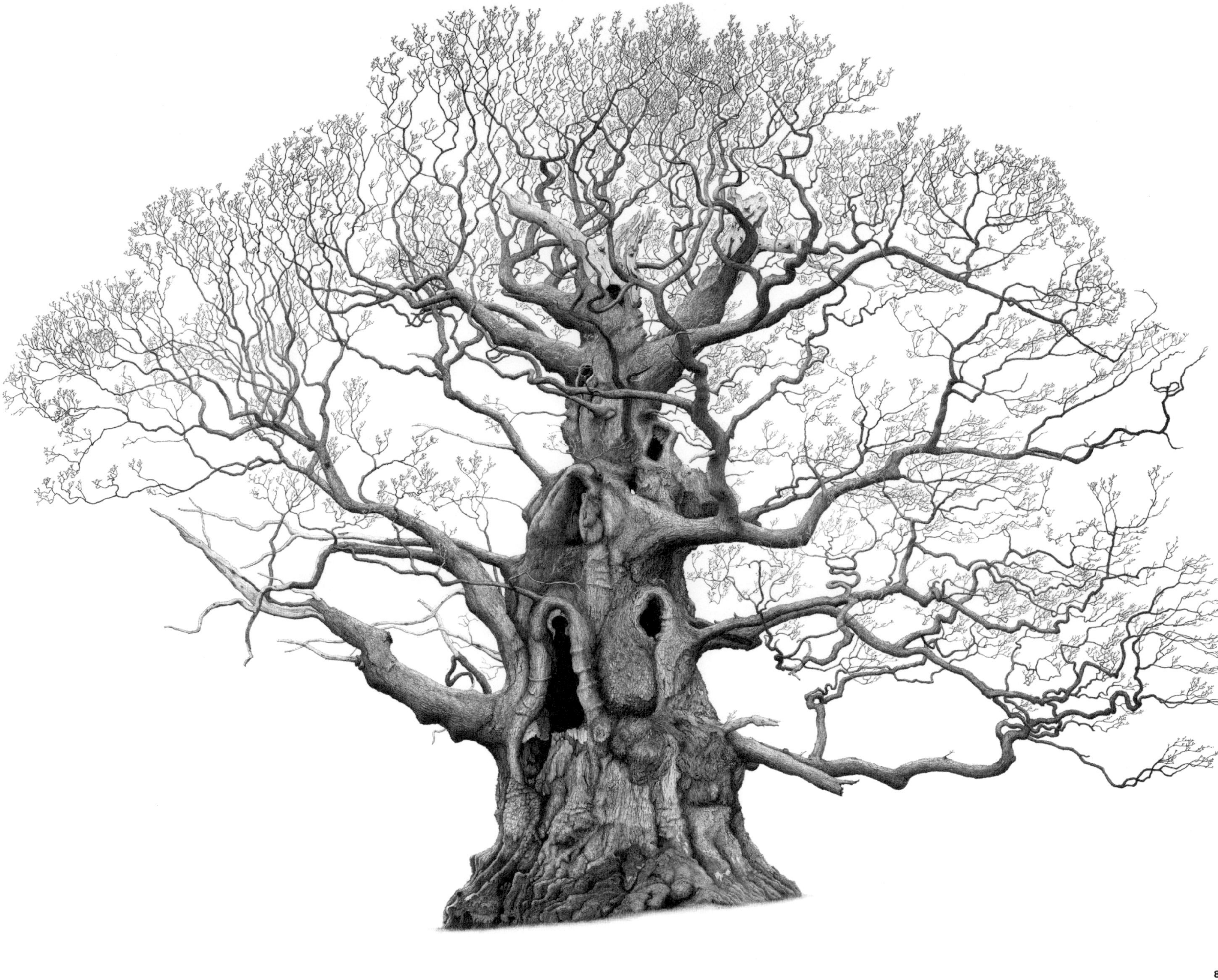

One impulse from a vernal wood
May teach you more of man,
Of moral evil and of good,
Than all the ages can.

William Wordsworth
The Tables Turned

Majesty or Fredville Oak
Detail

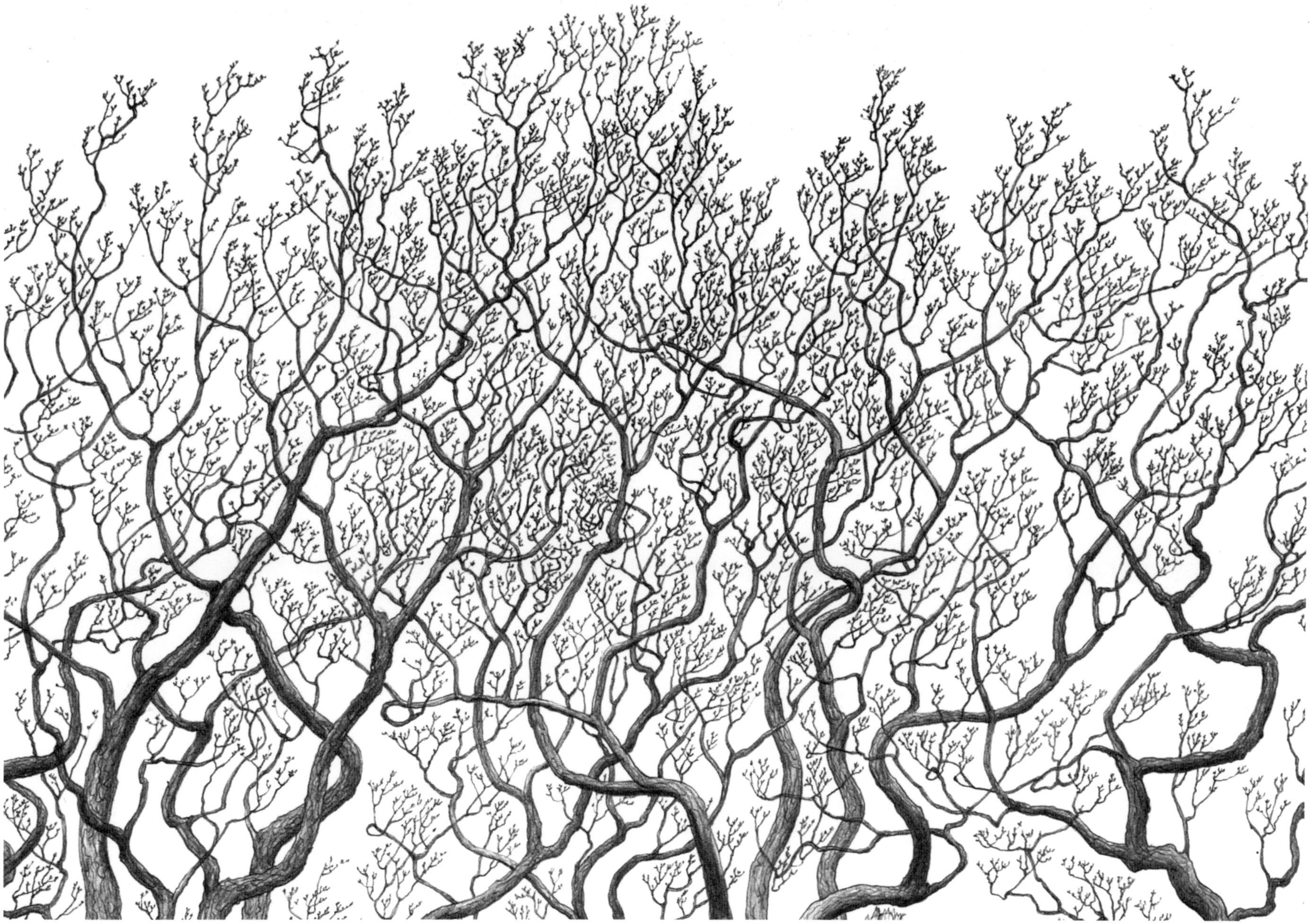

King Offa's Oak
Berkshire
Quercus robur
Graphite on paper
150 × 120 cm
2012

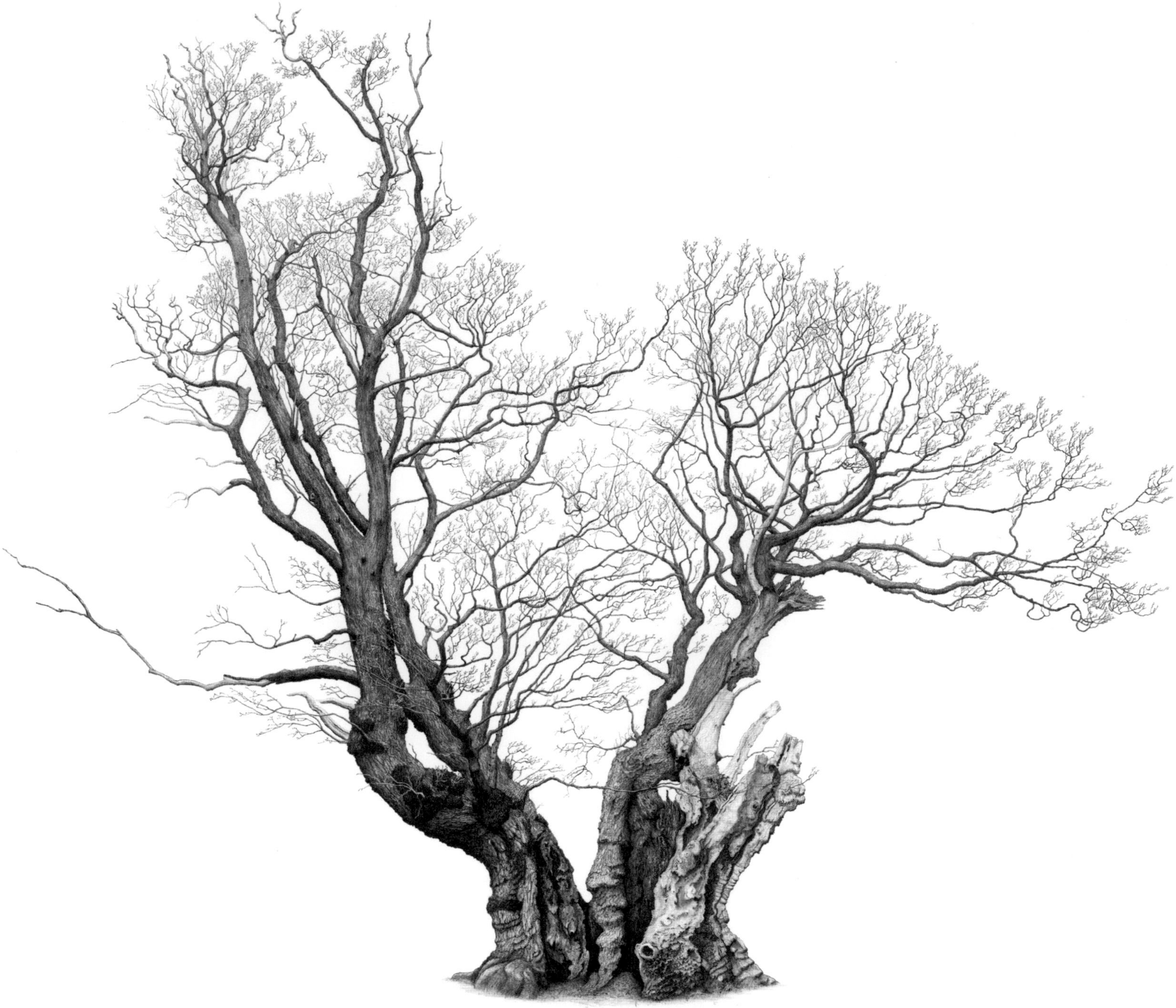

Majesty or Fredville Oak
Kent
Quercus robur
Graphite on paper
150 × 120 cm
2014

King Offa's Oak
Detail

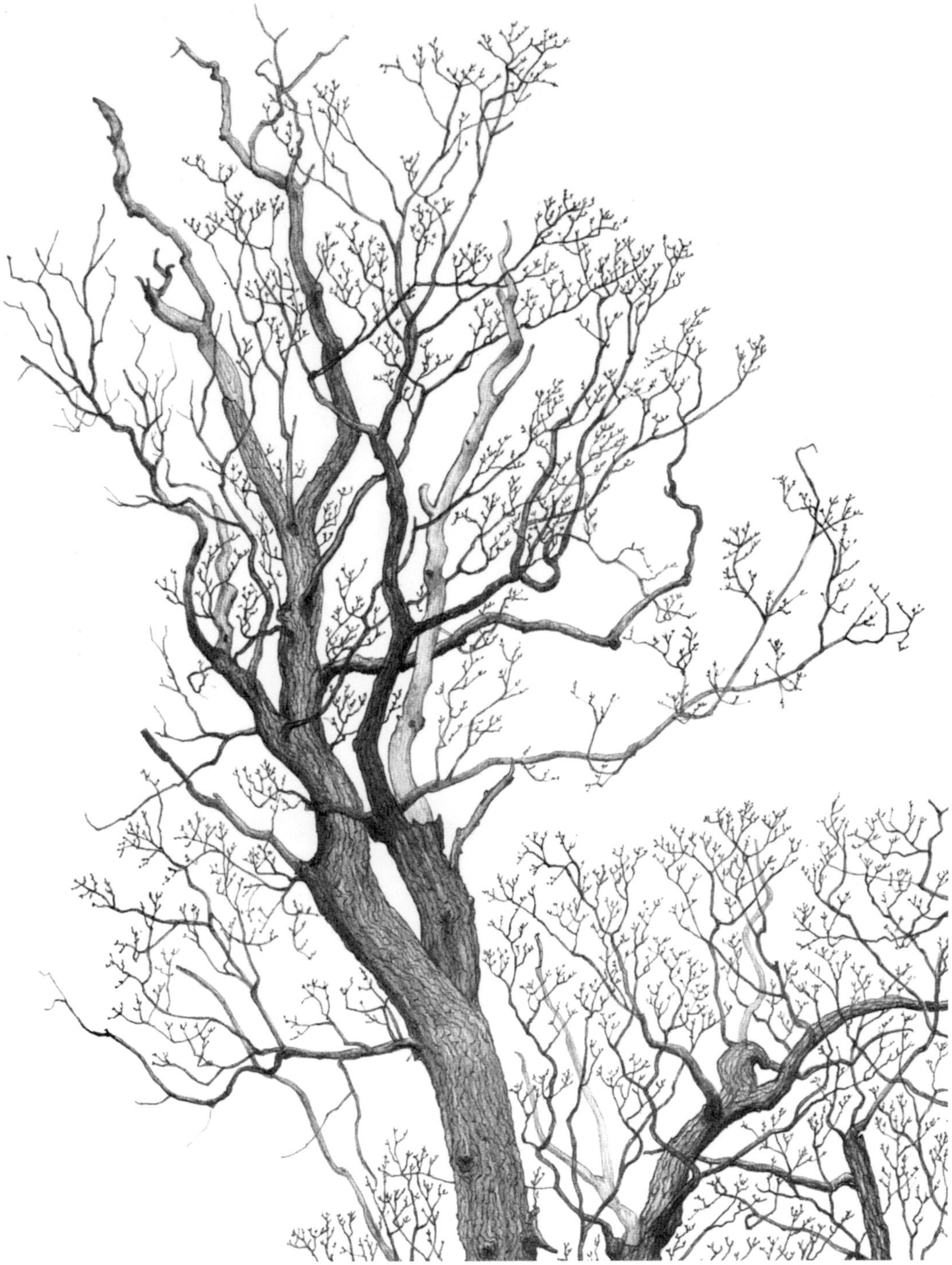

Jack of Kent's Oak
Herefordshire
Quercus robur
Graphite on paper
150 × 120 cm
2013

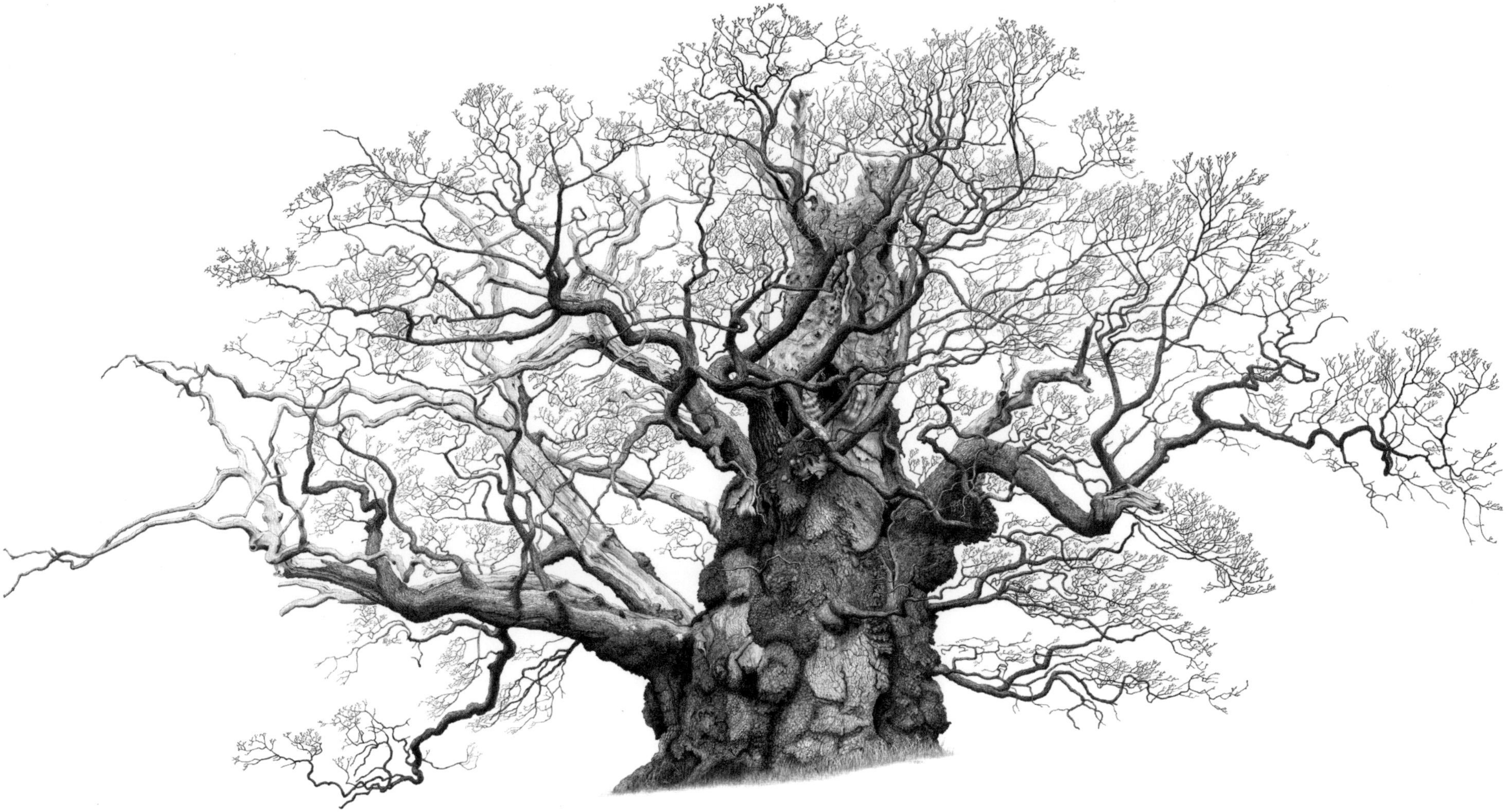

The Monarch Oak , the patriarch of trees,
Shoots rising up, and spreads by slow degrees.
Three centuries he grows, and three he stays,
Supreme in state, and in three more decays.

John Dryden
Palamon and Arcite

Jack of Kent's Oak
Detail

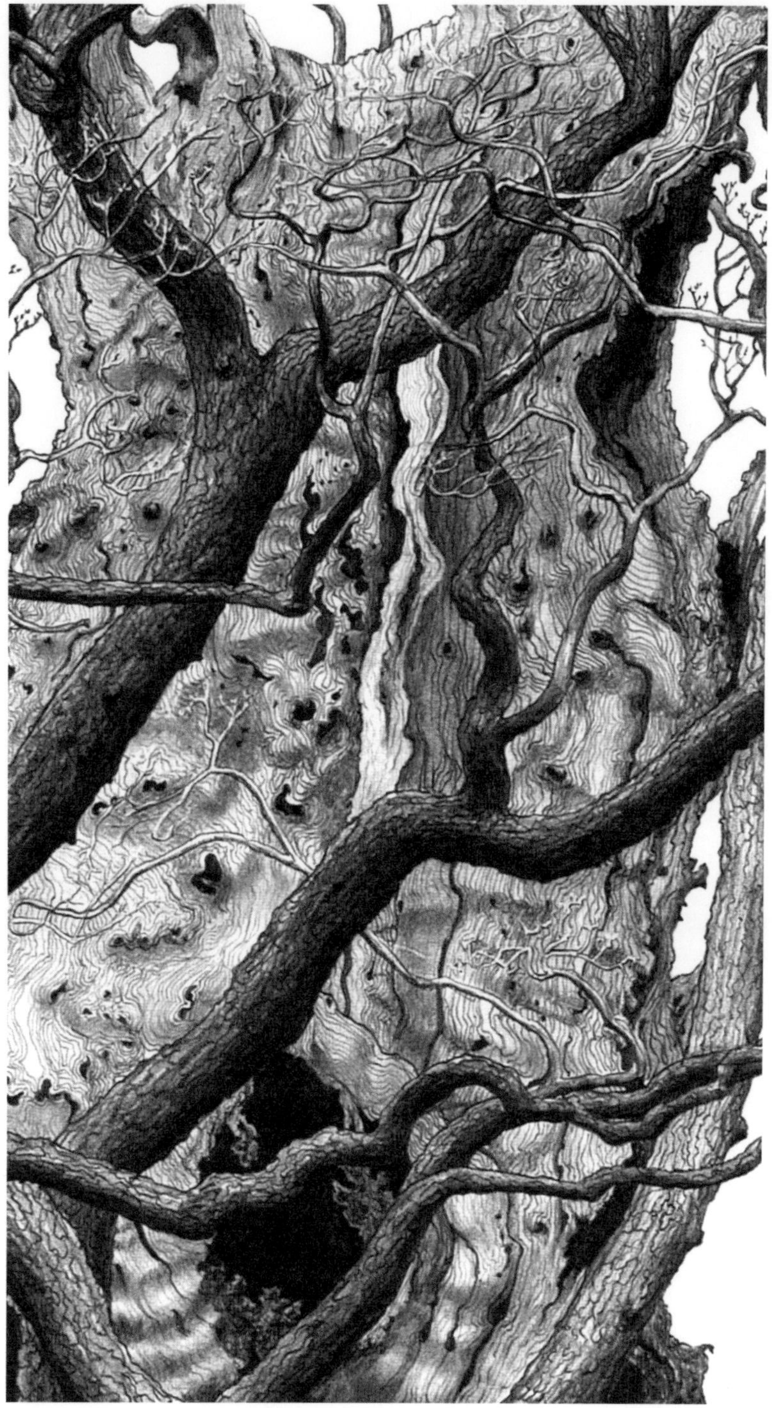

The Kedleston Hall Oak
Derbyshire
Quercus robur
Graphite on paper
150 × 120 cm
2018

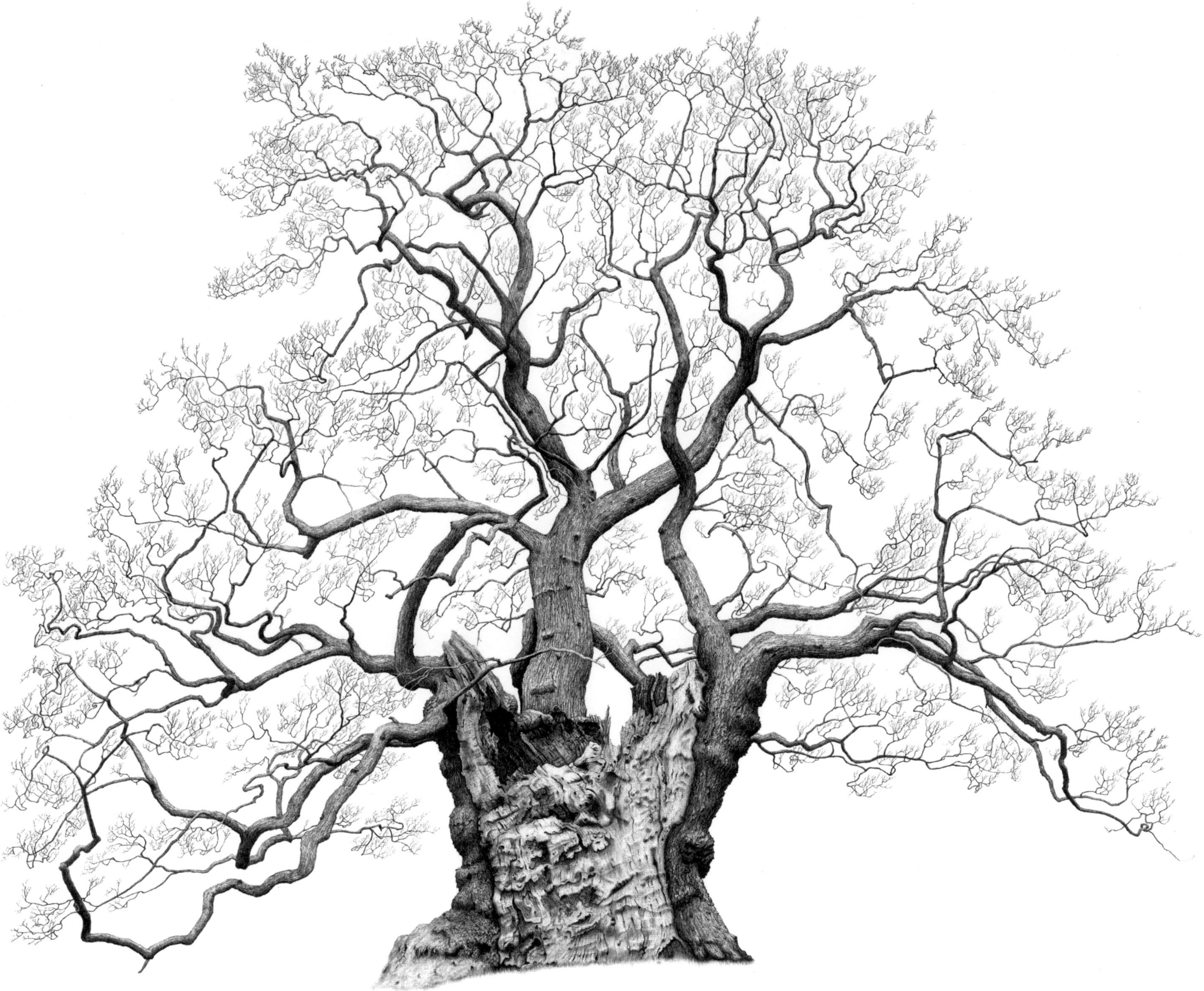

I wish that men now serving the great polished wheels, and works in iron and steel and brass could somehow be spared an hour to sit under this ancient oak … and come to know from the actual touch of its rugged bark that the past is living now.

Richard Jefferies
The Hills and the Vale

The Kedleston Hall Oak
Detail

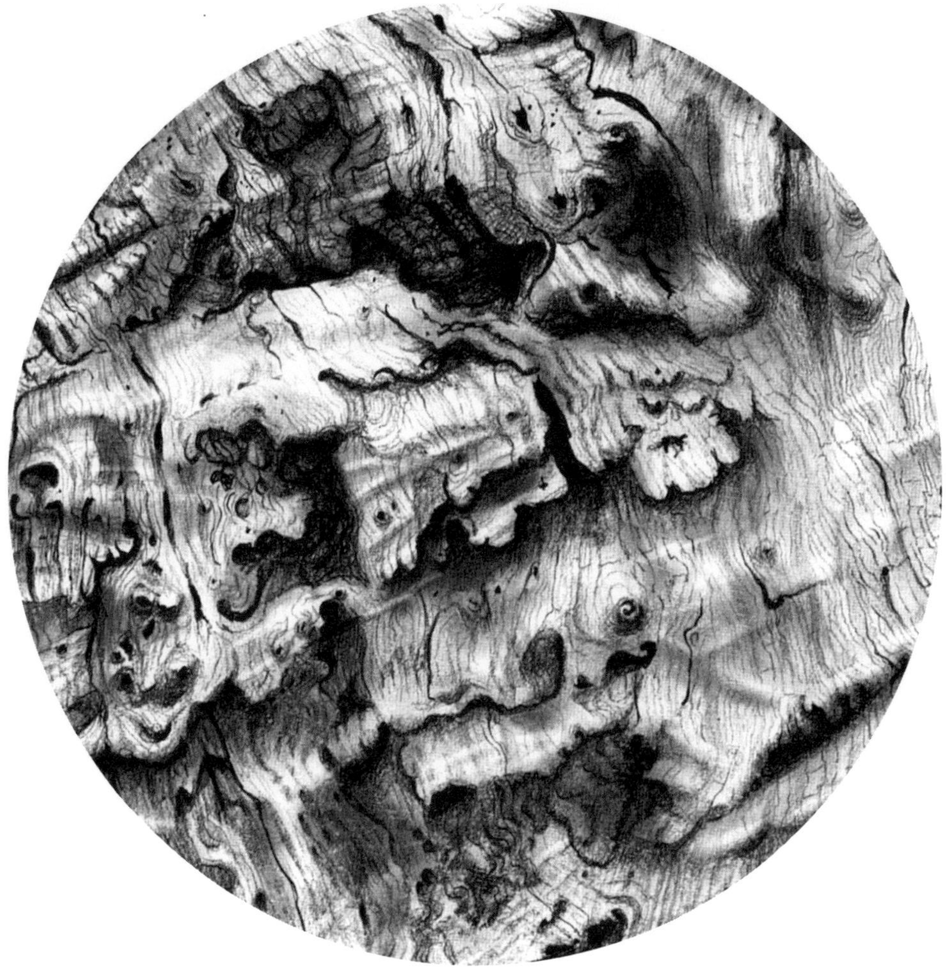

The Lydham Manor Oak
Shropshire
Quercus robur
Graphite on paper
150 × 120 cm
2015

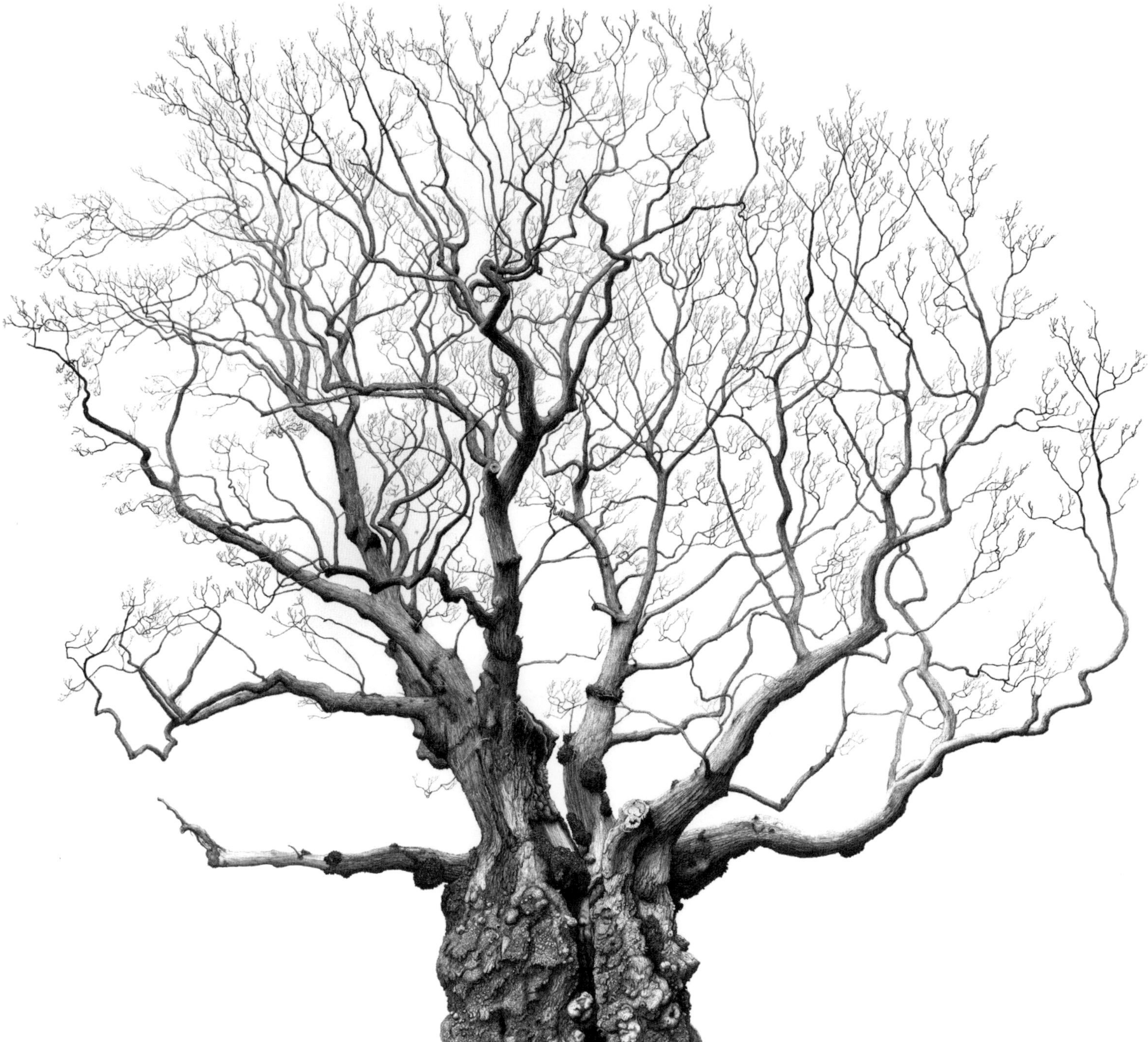

The Lydham Manor Oak
Detail

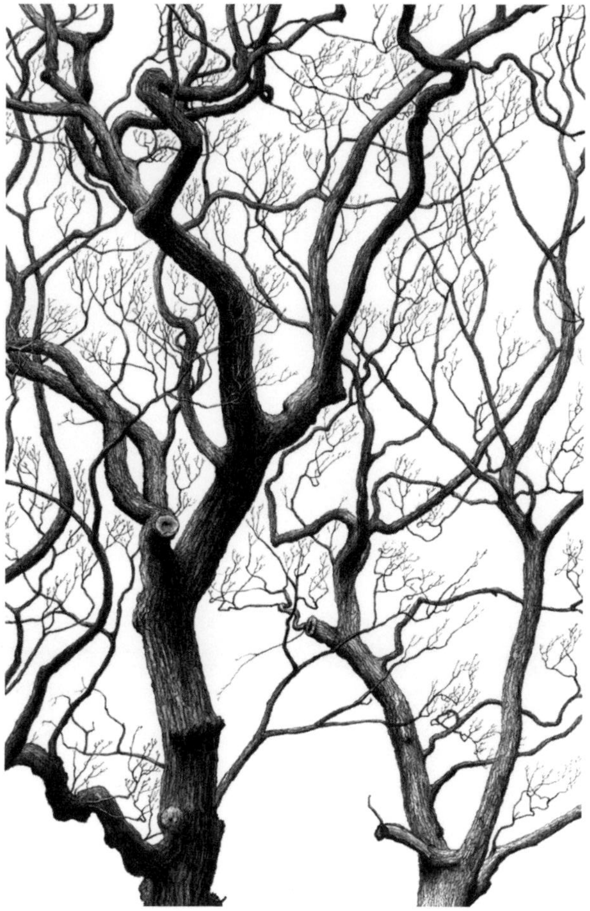

This comparatively young, though handsome pollarded oak grows in a hedgerow on the Spernal Estate in Warwickshire, now part of the Heart of England Forest. It is perhaps 150 years old. I included it in my series of drawings to offer a glimpse of the earlier years through which all ancient oaks must pass on their perilous journey down the centuries.

Mark Frith

The Spernal Oak
Warwickshire
Quercus robur
Graphite on paper
150 × 120 cm
2014

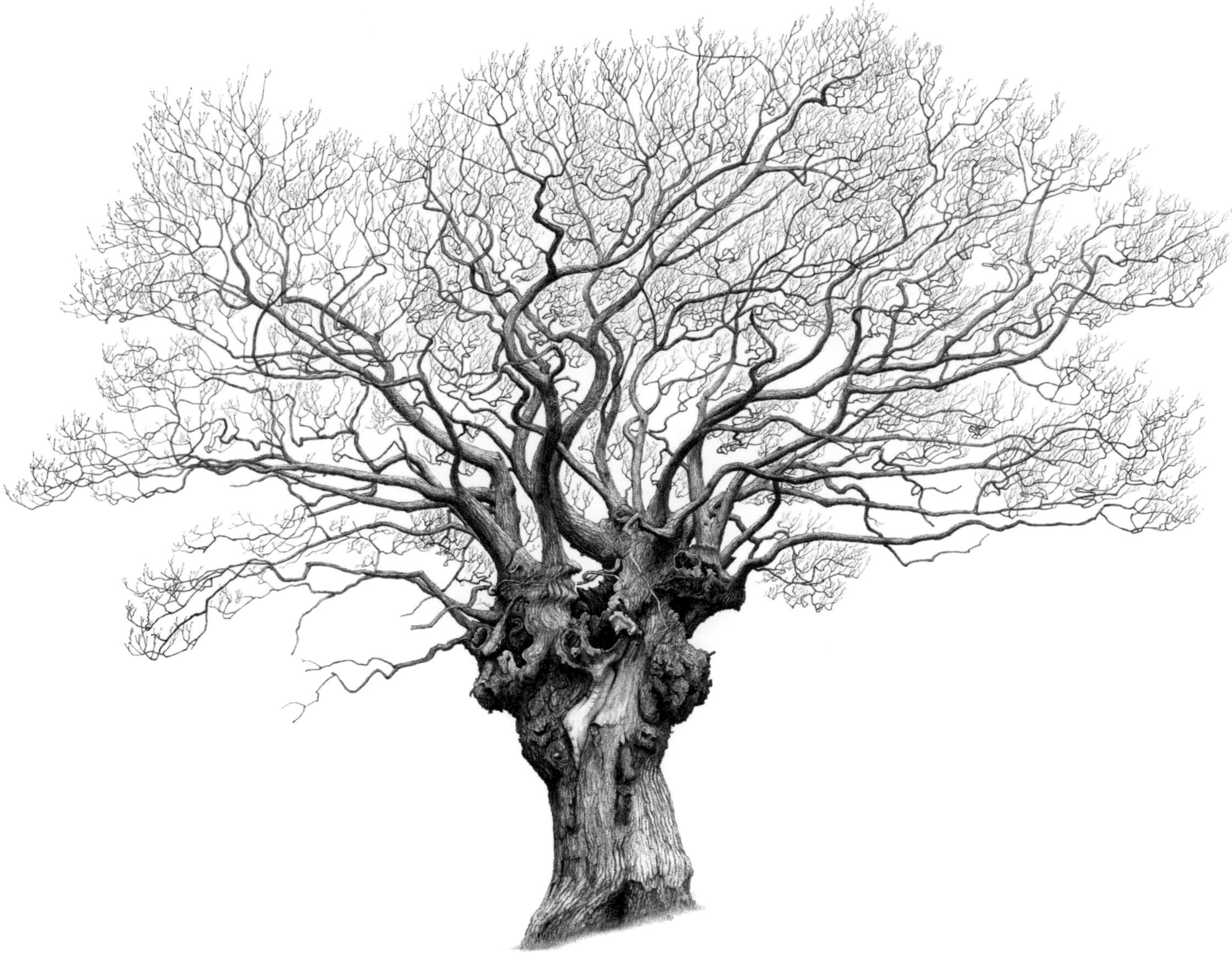

Then sing for the Oak Tree,
The monarch of the wood;
Sing for the Oak Tree,That groweth green and good;
That groweth broad and branching
Within the forest shade;
That groweth now, and yet shall grow,
When we are lowly laid!

Mary Howitt
The Oak Tree

The Spernal Oak
Detail

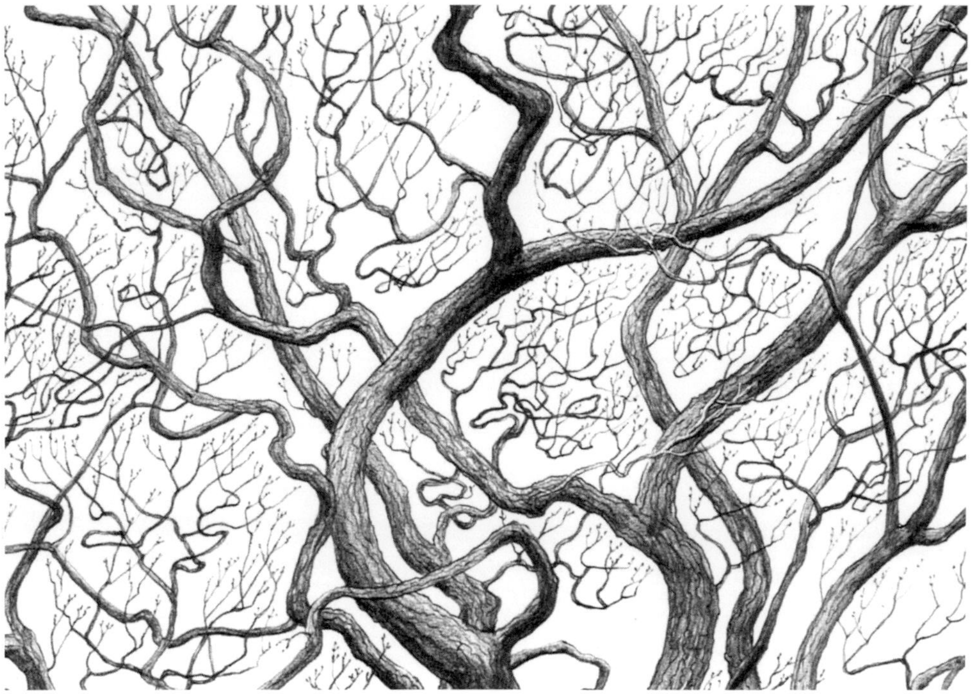

Gazetteer

When selecting which of Britain's most ancient oaks to include in this series of drawings, the guardians and fans of each individual tree, almost without exception, told me that their oak was considered the oldest in Britain and was certainly over one thousand years old. Due to their habit of hollowing out from the centre of the trunk, it is impossible to put an accurate age on ancient oaks. Dendrologists incline towards the opinion that all the trees included in this book, with the exception of the pollarded Spernal Oak, are in excess of five hundred years old. The majority are thought to be approaching one thousand years, with perhaps one or two being in their second millennium.

The majority of these trees are pollards, which means that throughout their life their branches have been regularly harvested for timber. Pollarding does not appear to have inhibited their lifespans. The minority of the trees which remain un-pollarded are referred to as maidens.

In selecting trees I took advice from many informed sources including the Ancient Tree Forum, The Tree Council, the Woodland Trust and, in particular, from tree photographer Archie Miles, whose encyclopaedic knowledge of Britain's notable trees was invaluable.

The individual trees are scattered from Cornwall to the Scottish Borders and from Lincolnshire to North Wales. Some are in public spaces but the majority grow on private land where permission is required to visit.

At the time of publication (2018) all the trees are still standing with the exception, alas, of the Pontfadog oak, which was felled by a northerly gale in April 2013.

Mark Frith

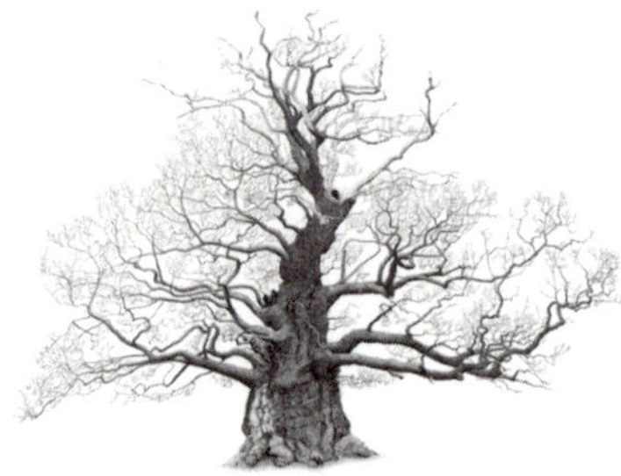

The Great Oak at Nibley Green
Gloucestershire
Quercus robur
Girth: 10.50 m
Maiden
Private land

Located at Nibley Green adjoining the village of North Nibley in Gloucestershire, this tree is thought to have witnessed the last battle fought on English soil between two private armies, in 1470. It stands on what was once the eastern edge of Michaelwood, which was used as cover for a surprise attack during the battle. This is the tree which inspired Mark Frith's series of drawings. He was moved to draw it following the rekindling of childhood memories of playing inside its hollow trunk.

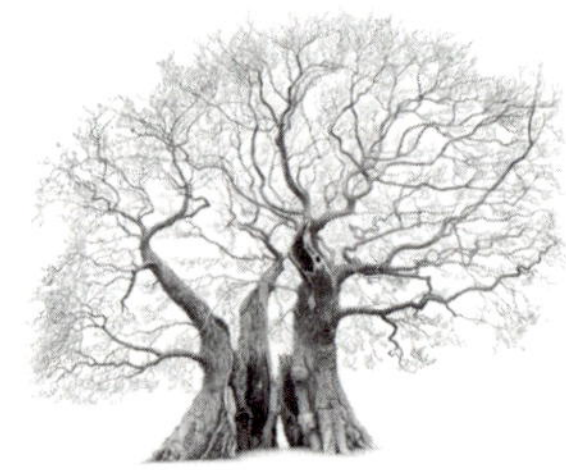

The Marton Oak
Cheshire
Quercus petraea
Girth: 14.02 m
Pollard
Private land

Located in a private garden in Oak Lane, Marton, in Cheshire, for several centuries this tree has laid claim to being one of Britain's largest oaks. In the past it has been used as a goose enclosure, bull enclosure, store for agricultural equipment, and, more recently, a bespoke Wendy house. The trunk has split into three separate fragments, which are now leaning outward due to increasing weight in the now un-pollarded crown.

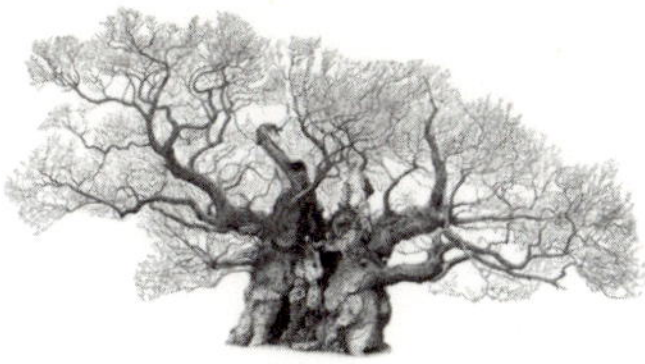

The Bowthorpe Oak
Lincolnshire
Quercus robur
Girth: 12.08 m
Pollard
Private land

Located in Manthorpe near Bourne in Lincolnshire, its fans make the oft-repeated claim that this is England's oldest oak, estimating its age to be over one thousand years. It too has served as a pen to various farmyard animals. At one time the hollow interior was fitted with seats and is said to have been used as a dining room for twenty people. Selected by The Tree Council in 2002 as one of fifty great British trees in honour of the Queen's Golden Jubilee. The Bowthorpe oak has also featured in the Guinness World Records.

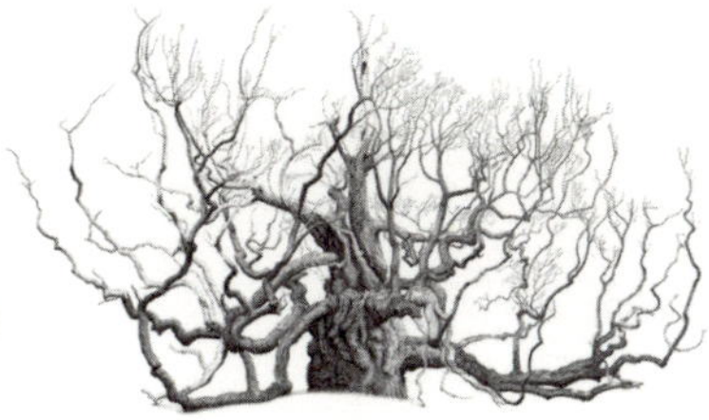

The King John Oak
Devon
Quercus robur
Girth: 10.04 m
Pollard
Private land

Located in Woodend Park in Shute, Devon, it is the largest of many ancient oaks in this former medieval deer park. It is named after King John (reigned 1199–1216). Tradition has it that the tree grew from an acorn planted by the King when out hunting. Neglect has allowed the once pollarded crown to run rampant, creating a bizarre octopus-like limb structure.

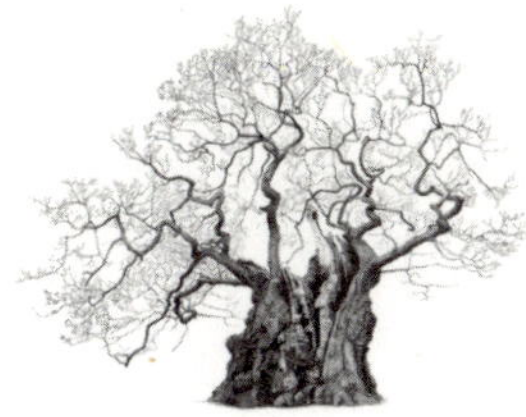

The Old Man of Calke
Derbyshire
Quercus robur
Girth: 10.01 m
Pollard
The National Trust

One of over two hundred ancient oaks scattered throughout the six hundred acres of ancient pastureland at Calke Abbey in Derbyshire, an estate which includes some of the rarest woodland habitats in Britain. Although once again believed by its fans to be over one thousand years old, the tree still produces acorns. When Calke became a National Nature Reserve in 2006, a competition was launched to name its oldest tree, the winning name being the Old Man of Calke.

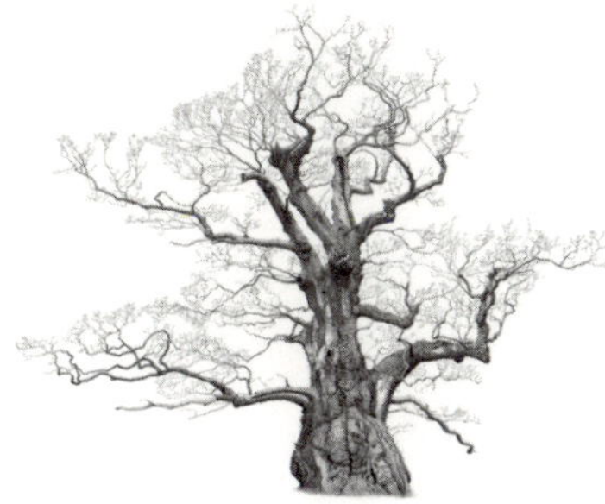

Billy Wilkins
Dorset
Quercus robur
Girth: 11.92 m
Maiden
Private land

Located in Melbury Park, Dorset, the tree has acquired the unusual name of Billy Wilkins, thought to be the namesake of a steward from the estate in the late seventeenth century. In his *Dendrologia* (1827), James Mitchell describes it as being 'as curly, surly, knotty an old monster as can be conceived'. Thomas Hardy refers to it in *The Woodlanders*, as 'Great Willy, the largest oak in the wood'. Henry John Elwes and Augustine Henry visited it for their *The Trees of Great Britain and Ireland* (1906–1913), which includes a beautiful photogravure plate of the tree.

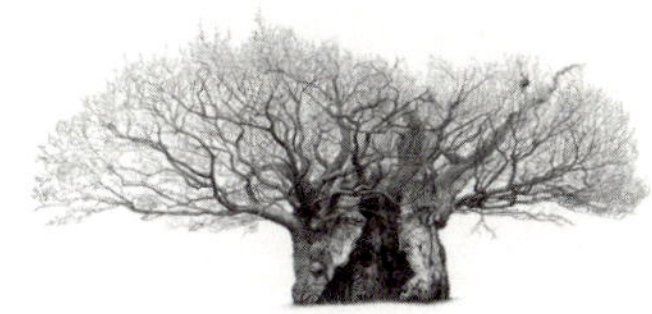

Queen Elizabeth I Oak
Sussex
Quercus petraea
Girth: 12.67 m
Pollard (natural)
The Cowdray Park Estate

Located in Cowdray Park near the village of Lodsworth in the Sussex Weald, it is the third largest sessile oak to be recorded in Britain, after the Pontfadog Oak in Wales and the Marton Oak in Cheshire. According to legend Queen Elizabeth I stood under this tree, with an arrow ready in her bow, waiting for a stag to be driven within range for her to shoot. The royal huntress was apparently unsuccessful in her hunt. The Tree Council designated the Queen Elizabeth I oak one of fifty great British trees in recognition of its place in the national heritage.

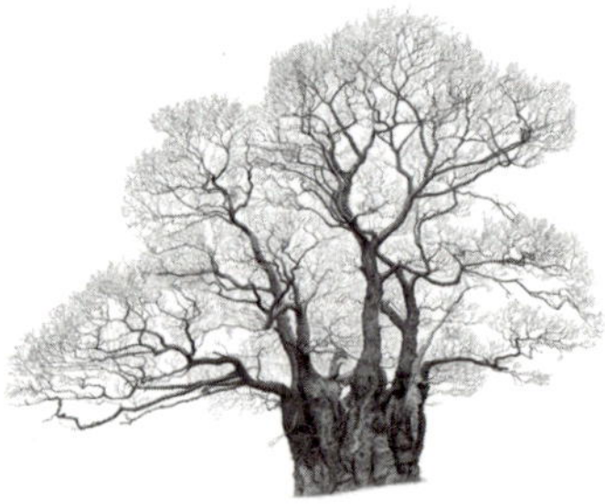

The Gospel Oak
Herefordshire
Quercus robur
Girth:12.80 m
Pollard
Private land

Located near Newbury Farm in Grendon Bishop, Herefordshire, the Gospel Oak is one of many gigantic English oaks which came to widespread notice through the Ancient Tree Hunt, a partnership project between the Tree Register of the British Isles and the Woodland Trust starting in 2005. Its name is a reference to the gospel meetings thought to have been held beside it. The trunk has decayed into four segments, which are now leaning outwards under the weight of the now un-pollarded crown.

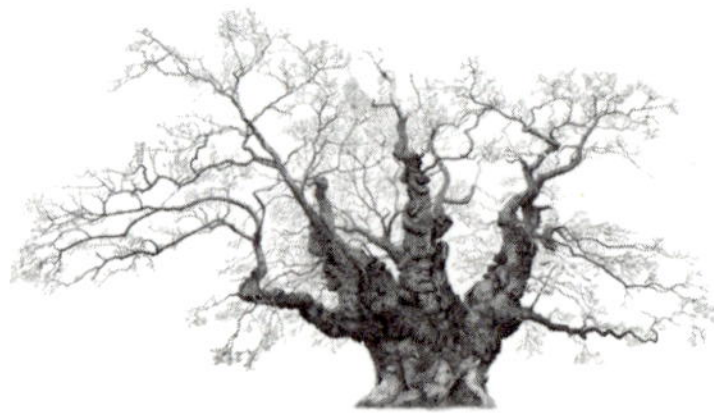

The Mottisfont or Oakley Oak
Hampshire
Quercus robur
Girth: 10.74 m
Pollard
The National Trust

Located in a water meadow on the banks of the River Test, the tree stands near to the original site of an Augustinian priory founded in 1201 by William Briwere. During the dissolution of the monasteries under Henry VIII, the priory was dissolved and the King gave Mottisfont to a favoured statesman, Sir William Sandys, who turned it into a country home. Inclusion within this private estate gave the tree the protection needed to survive down the centuries.

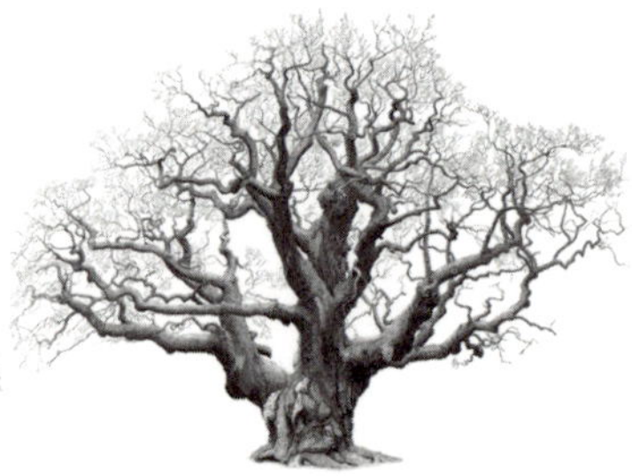

The Major Oak
Nottinghamshire
Quercus robur
Girth: 10.66 m
Pollard
The Forestry Commission

Located in Sherwood Forest, the legendary stomping ground of Robin Hood. One of many hundreds of old oaks in the forest, its earliest recorded name, from the mid-1800s, is the Cockpen Tree, as the sport of cock fighting took place beneath its boughs. In 1790, Major Hayman Rooke, a noted archaeologist, included the tree in his popular book about the ancient oaks of Sherwood, hence its name. Conservation measures, carried out continually since 1908, have created a somewhat surreal Daliesque framework of crutches and wires throughout the tree, which Mark Frith chose to exclude from his drawing.

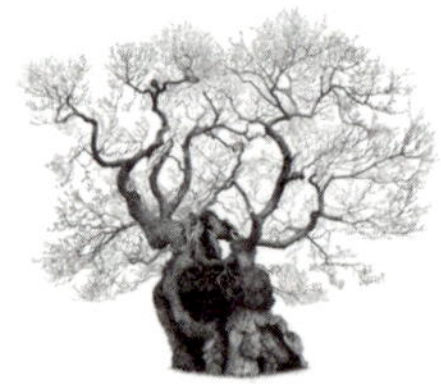

Judge Wyndham's Oak
Dorset
Quercus robur
Girth: 9.86 m
Pollard
Private land

Also known as the Silton Oak, as it is located in the Dorset village of Silton. It stands in a meadow behind St Nicholas' parish church and is named after Sir Hugh Wyndham, a seventeenth-century judge whose career spanned the rules of Charles I, the Commonwealth and Charles II. According to local legend, Sir Hugh often sat in the shade of this great tree. Thought to be more than a thousand years old, it may have been a boundary marker of the Gillingham Forest, a royal deer hunting chase favoured by King John. It was also used as a 'hanging tree' or gibbet by the notorious 'Hanging' Judge Jeffreys.

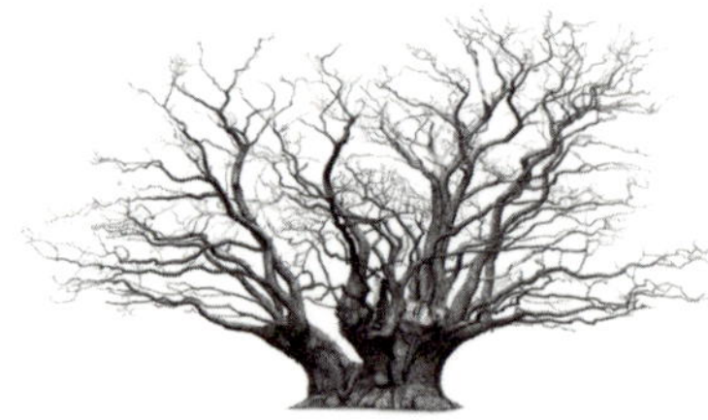

The Chaceley Oak
Gloucestershire
Quercus robur
Girth: 12.51 m
Pollard (dead)
Private land

Located on the floodplain of the River Severn close to the village of the same name, five miles from Tewkesbury. The tree appears to have died in the last decade, possibly as a result several recent periods of prolonged flooding from the River Severn. Deep ploughing of the surrounding field may also have contributed to its demise.

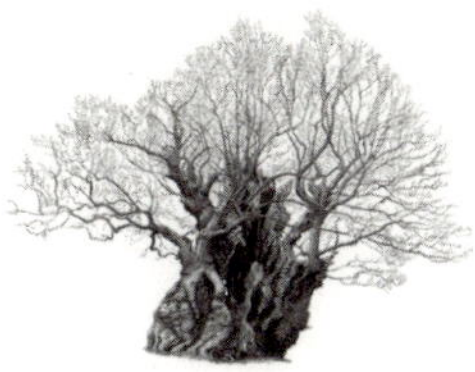

The Pontfadog Oak
Powys
Quercus petraea
Girth:12.85 m
Pollard (dead and fallen)
No longer standing

The Pontfadog oak stood on Cilcochwyn Farm above the village of Pontfadog, near Chirk in North Wales. It was blown over in the early hours of 18 April 2013. Reputed by some to be the oldest and largest oak in the United Kingdom, it was estimated to be over a thousand years old. Known as Wales's national tree, legend claims that Welsh princes once rallied their troops beside it. Its hollow trunk was said to be big enough to seat six people at a table.

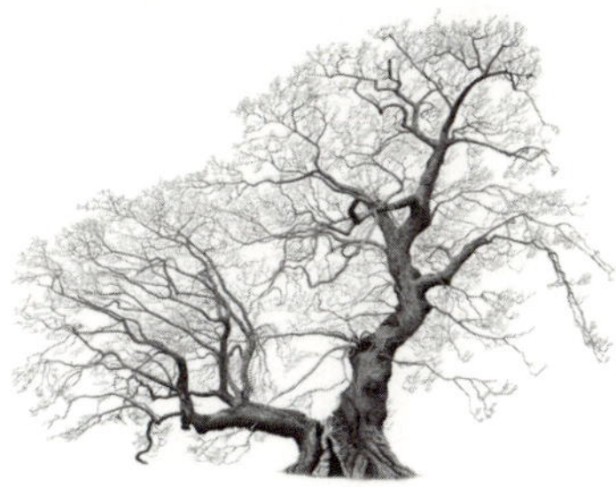

The Capon Oak
Scottish Borders
Quercus petraea
Girth: 9.74 m
Possible pollard
Public access on roadside verge

Located two miles south of Jedburgh in Scotland, almost on the verge of the A68, this wide-spreading oak is known as King of the Woods. It is one of the last surviving trees from the ancient Jedforest that straddled the Scottish Borders, and is claimed by its fans to be over one thousand years old. The tree has split severely down the centre of its trunk and is held together with concrete, brick and timber beams, which Mark Frith chose to exclude from his drawing.

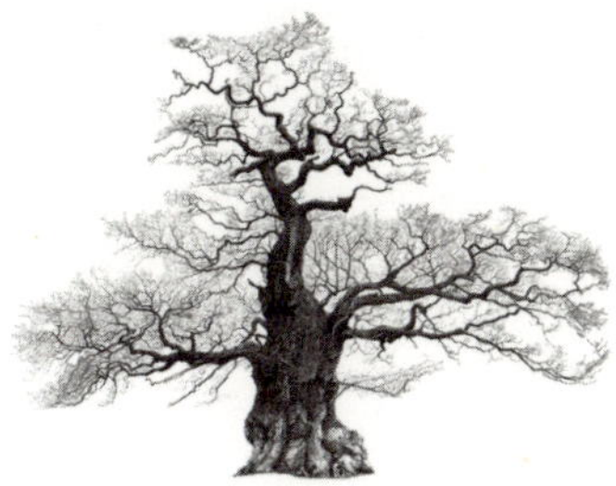

The Eastcourt Oak
Wiltshire
Quercus robur
Girth: 8.30 m
Maiden
Private land

Located in a water meadow immediately in front of Eastcourt House, near the village of that name. In medieval times the entire parish of Eastcourt was the property of Benedictine monks from nearby Malmesbury Abbey. The tree's intimate association with Eastcourt House, built in 1658, seems likely to have provided the continued protection needed to enable this veteran oak to survive to this day. Home to wild bees and barn owls, ribbons are still tied to its boughs by supplicants hoping for good luck.

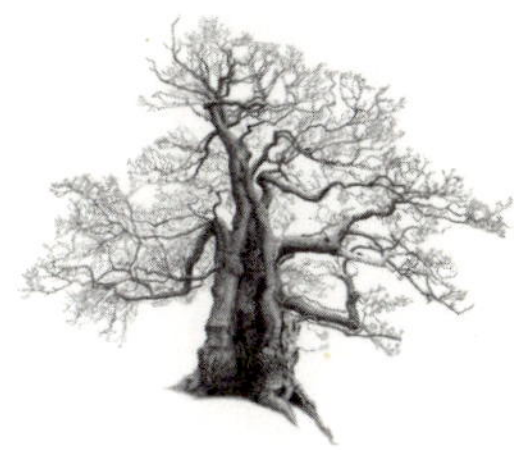

The Darley Oak
Cornwall
Quercus robur
Girth: 11.60 m
Maiden
Private land

Standing near the village of Upton Cross in the private garden of Darley Farm, this tree is thought to be around one thousand years old. Folk tradition attributes healing properties to the tree, and it is said that any wish made to it will eventually come true. Its acorns are used as amulets, and were once used by pregnant women to bring them luck. Despite losing half its trunk to storm damage in recent decades the tree is thought to be in good health, although it may not grow any larger.

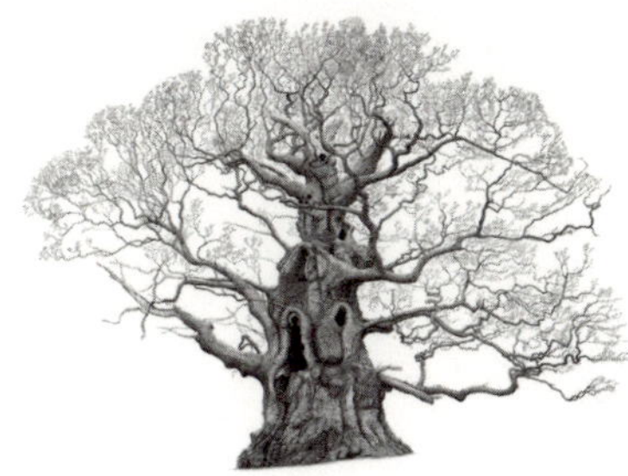

Majesty or Fredville Oak
Kent
Quercus robur
Girth: 12.18 m
Maiden
Private land

Located in Fredville Park, Nonington, near Dover. Since the late eighteenth century the park has been renowned for its magnificent trees, especially oaks and chestnuts. The Fredville Oak, also known as Majesty, is seen by many as the most impressive oak in Britain. It is one of the biggest and also a healthy maiden tree with a tall trunk and still substantial crown. In the early twentieth century it lost an enormous limb about four metres up the trunk, which revealed the tree to be totally hollow. It is most likely over one thousand years old.

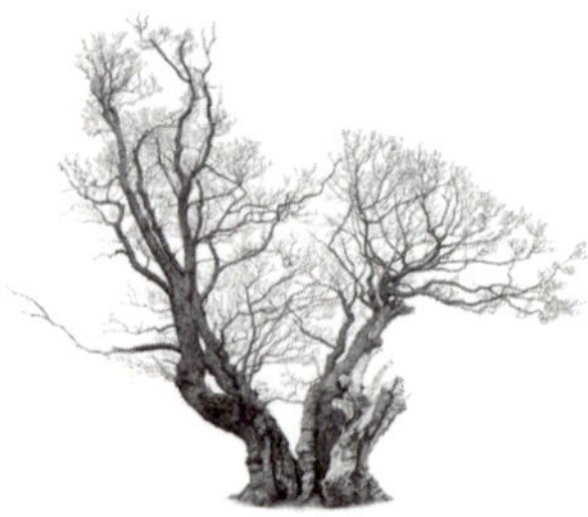

King Offa's Oak
Berkshire
Quercus robur
Girth: 11.18 m
Pollard
Crown Estates

King Offa's Oak is located in Windsor Great Park, which contains one of the largest numbers of ancient oaks in western Europe. At over one thousand years in age, it is believed to be older than Windsor Castle. Its several limbs have splayed outward severely and are supported by timber props, which Mark Frith has excluded from his drawing.

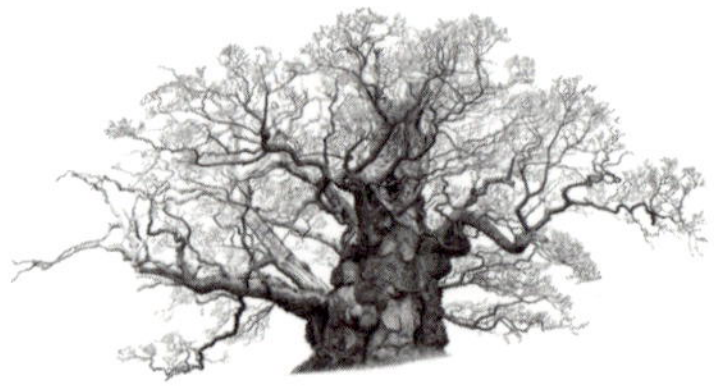

Jack of Kent's Oak
Herefordshire
Quercus robur
Girth: 11.37 m
Pollard
Private land

Growing in the medieval deer park at Kentchurch Court in Herefordshire, a former hunting park originally belonging to the Knights Templar, the tree is named after Jack of Kent, a folklore character from the Welsh Marches. He is referred to as a cleric or wizard who regularly beat the devil in bets and games. In 1547 the Scudamores of Kentchurch bought the deer park from the Knights Hospitallers of the Commandery of Dinmore, and it remains in their family to this day.

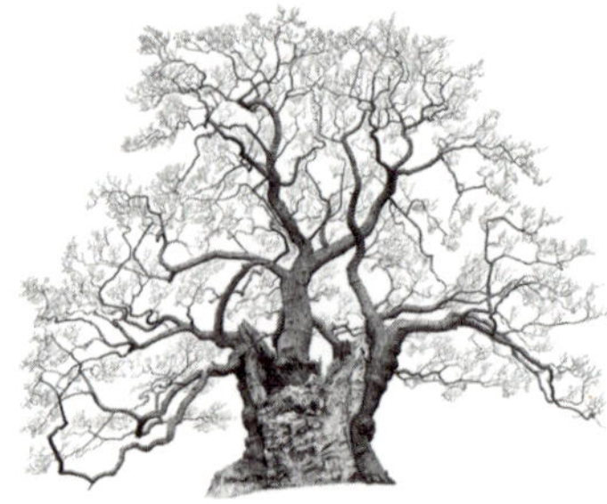

The Kedleston Hall Oak
Derbyshire
Quercus robur
Girth: 8.37 m
Pollard
The National Trust

Standing in a former medieval deer park, which in 1758 was remodelled in the Romantic style by architect and landscape designer Robert Adam for his employer Nathaniel Curzon. The gardens and grounds remain largely unaltered to this day. Parts of the estate are a designated Site of Special Scientific Interest, primarily because of the 'rich and diverse deadwood invertebrate fauna' inhabiting its ancient oaks.

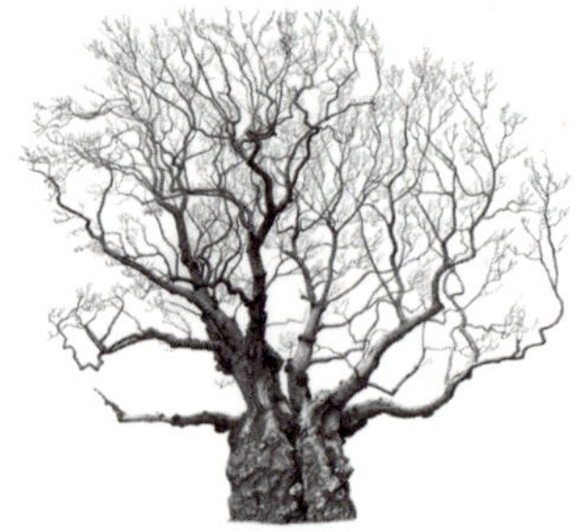

The Lydham Manor Oak
Shropshire
Quercus robur
Girth: 13.01 m
Pollard
Private land

Standing in the park of Lydham Manor near Bishop's Castle, Shropshire. The trunk is heavily burred and still grows vigorously. Repeated measurements since 1940 suggest this impressive tree may in fact be no more than three hundred years old.

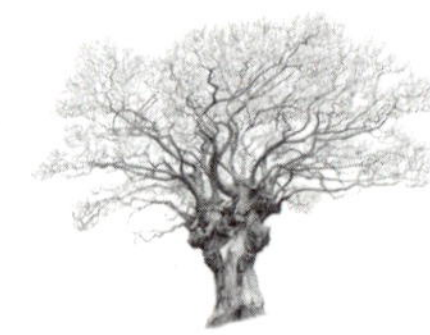

The Spernal Oak
Warwickshire
Quercus robur
Girth: 5.50 m
Pollard
The Heart of England Forest

Located in Spernal Park, part of the Heart of England Forest which stretches from the ancient borders of Shakespeare's Forest of Arden to the edge of the Vale of Evesham. Mark Frith included this comparatively young hedgerow pollard in his series to offer a glimpse of the earlier years through which all ancient oaks must pass. The Heart of England Forest's mission is to restore and rebuild some of England's lost ancient forest.

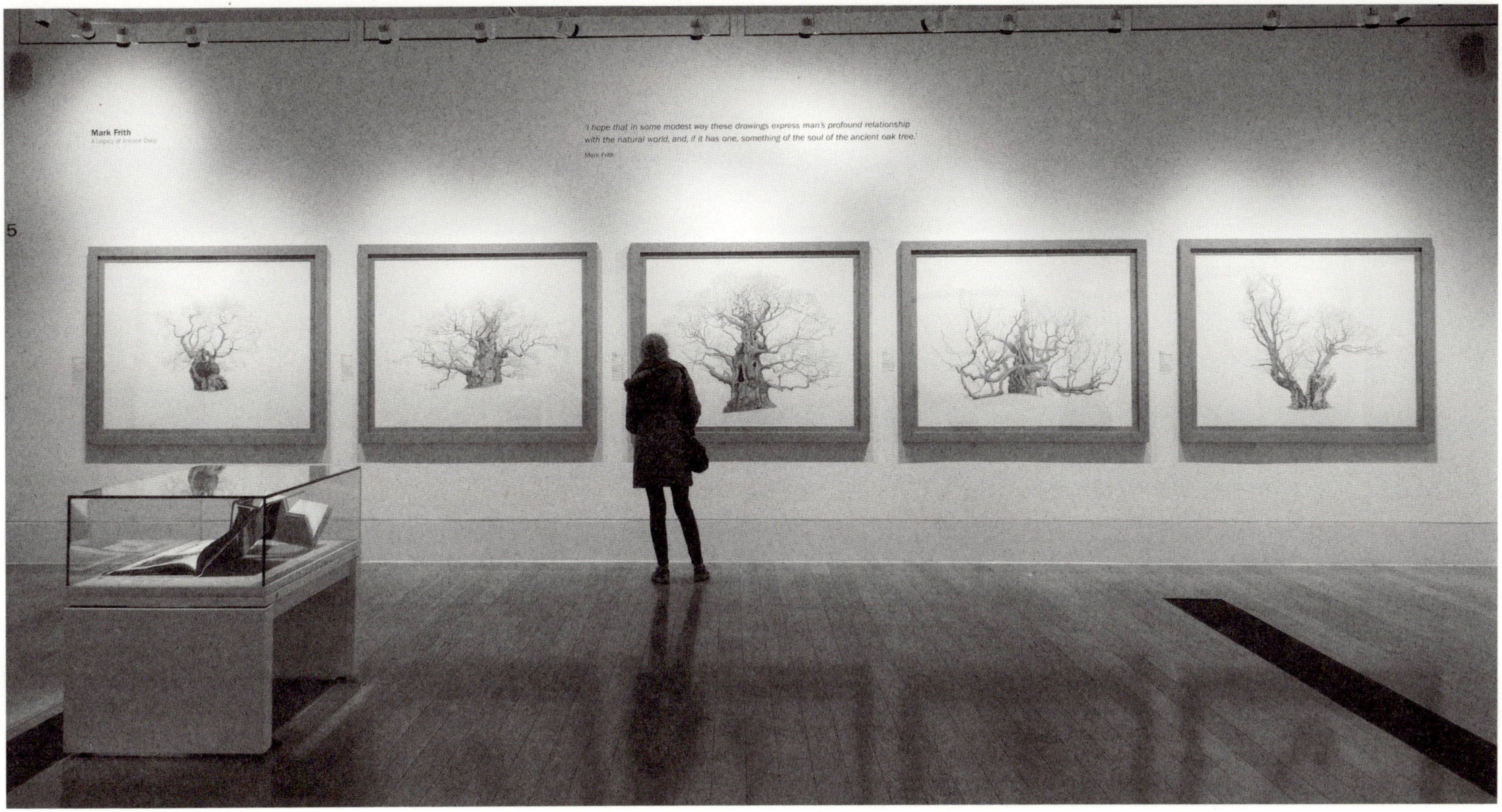

A Legacy of Ancient Oaks exhibition at the Shirley Sherwood Gallery, Kew October 2018 – March 2019
Photo by Jeff Eden © RBG Kew

Acknowledgements

I would like to thank the following parties for allowing me to draw trees on their land: the Marton Oak, Cheshire, Mrs Joan Fawcus; the Pontfadog Oak, Powys, Mr and Mrs Williams; the Gospel Oak, Herefordshire, Mr Jeremy Leigthon; the Lydham Manor Oak, Shropshire, Mr William Sykes; the Great Oak, Nibley Green, Gloucestershire, Mr and Mrs Nick Turk; the Bowthorpe Oak, Lincolnshire, Mrs Anne Blanchard; the Fredville Oak, Kent, Mr John Plumtree; King Offa's Oak, Windsor Great Park, Crown Estates; the Darley Oak, Cornwall, Mrs Hoare; Billy Wilkins, Dorset, the Honourable Charlotte Townsend; Jack of Kent's Oak, Herefordshire, Mrs Jan Lucas-Scudamore; the Mottisfont Oak, Hampshire, the Old Man of Calke, and the Kedleston Hall Oak, Derbyshire, the National Trust; the Major Oak, Nottinghamshire, the Forestry Commission; King John Oak, Devon, Mr John Bird and Mr Rick Wood; Queen Elizabeth Oak, Sussex, the Cowdray Estate; the Spernal Oak, The Heart of England Forest; the Eastcourt Oak, Wiltshire, Mr and Mrs James Reed.

In addition I would like to thank the following people for their help in completing this series of drawings and book: William Sieghart for his tip off; Archie Miles for his encyclopaedic knowledge; Lionel Rothschild and Dr Chris Mills for their assistance in liaising with the Royal Botanic Gardens, Kew; Dr Shirley Sherwood for her enthusiastic support; Pete Howells from Darbyshire framers; photographers Steve Russell and Ashley Hatton from Steve Russell Studios; Ian Leggett, Caroline Rush and staff from The Heart of England Forest; Maria Devaney for her curatorial work at the Shirley Sherwood Gallery and for her contribution to the Gazetteer; Gina Fullerlove, Georgie Hills, Lydia White, Christine Beard and Pei Chu at Kew Publishing; Aljos Farjon for his expert factual advice on the Gazetteer; and book designer Ocky Murray for his design skills and patience.

Finally I must thank Emma Crichton-Miller both for her written contribution to this book and for her unstinting critical and moral support throughout the project.

Mark Frith

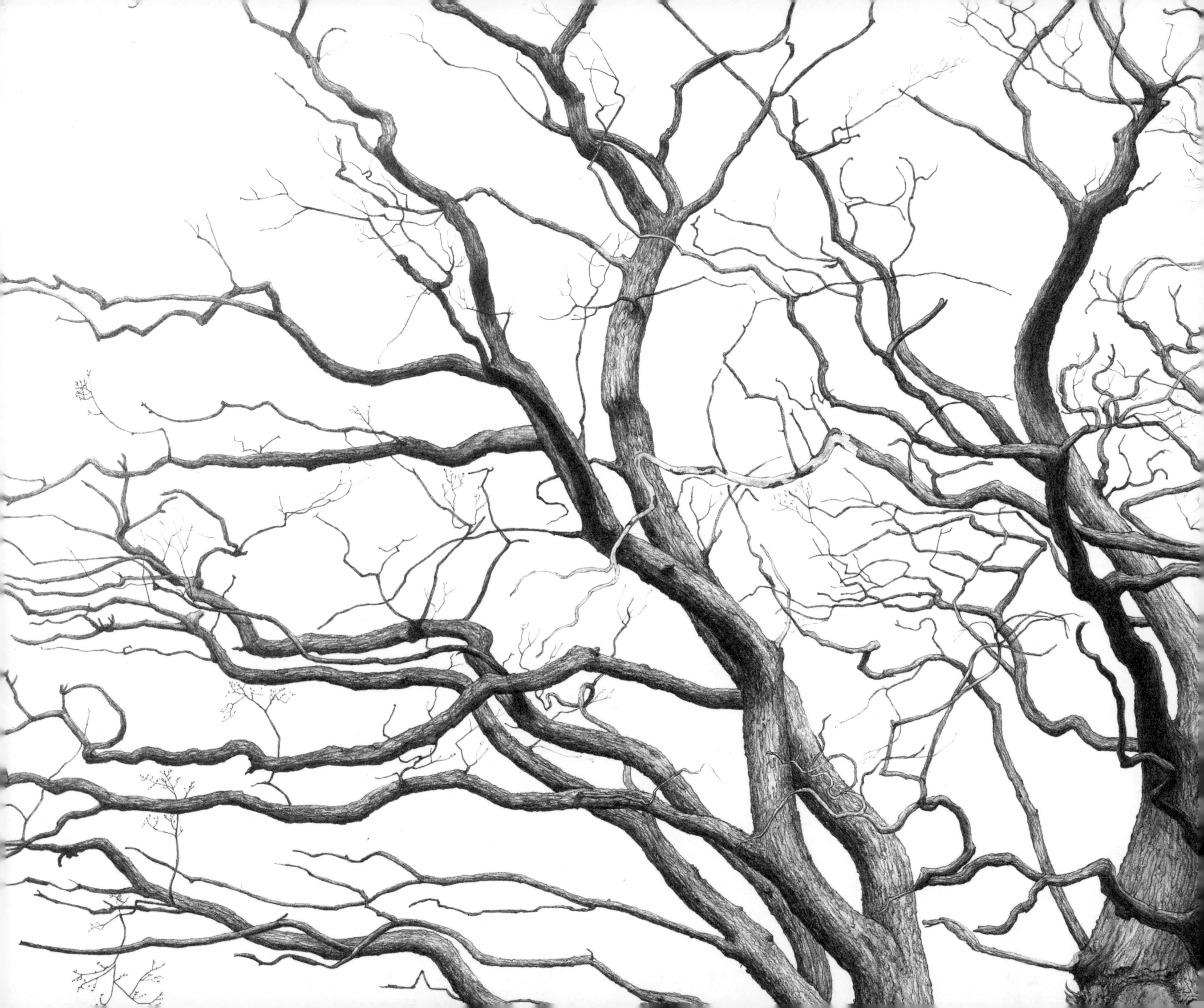